To Breathe with Birds

To Breathe with Birds

A Book of Landscapes

Václav Cílek

TRANSLATED BY Evan W. Mellander

PHOTOGRAPHS BY Morna Livingston

FOREWORD BY Laurie Olin

PENN

University of Pennsylvania Press *Philadelphia*

PENN STUDIES IN LANDSCAPE ARCHITECTURE

John Dixon Hunt, Series Editor

This series is dedicated to the study and promotion of a wide variety of approaches to landscape architecture, with special emphasis on connections between theory and practice. It includes monographs on key topics in history and theory, descriptions of projects by both established and rising designers, translations of major foreign-language texts, anthologies of theoretical and historical writings on classic issues, and critical writing by members of the profession of landscape architecture.

The series was the recipient of the Award of Honor in Communications from the American Society of Landscape Architects, 2006.

Publication of this work was assisted by a grant from the Centre for the Future.

Published by
University of Pennsylvania Press
Philadelphia, Pennsylvania 19104-4112
www.upenn.edu/pennpress

Printed in the United States of America on acid-free paper

10 9 8 7 6 5 4 3 2 1

Library of Congress Cataloging-in-Publication Data

Cílek, Václav.
  To breathe with birds : a book of landscapes / Václav Cílek ; translated by Evan W. Mellander ; photographs by Morna Livingston ; foreword by Laurie Olin. — 1st ed.
       p. cm. — (Penn studies in landscape architecture)
  Texts were originally written in Czech.
  ISBN 978-0-8122-4681-0
  1. Landscapes—Czech Republic—History. 2. Landscapes—Czech Republic—Bohemia—History. 3. Cultural landscapes. 4. Cultural geography. 5. Nature and civilization. 6. Czech Republic—Description and travel. 7. Bohemia (Czech Republic)—Description and travel. I. Livingston, Morna. II. Title. III. Series: Penn studies in landscape architecture.
  DB2012.C55 2015
  943.71—dc23   2014029017

Frontispiece: Cubist column, Prague

CONTENTS

FOREWORD

Laurie Olin

This collection of essays in words and images is rather like a mysterious boulder discovered in one's back garden. A meteor perhaps? Solid, composed of known elements, familiar enough, but an unexpected arrival with news of a world that lies elsewhere and possibly in another time. Yet here it is, oddly compelling.

Václav Cílek is a Czech geologist, writer-philosopher, popular science author, and translator of Tao and Zen texts, a teacher and public figure in his country. After spending part of his childhood in Tanzania, where his father was a geologist, he moved to Prague to study mining engineering. He graduated with degrees in geology from Charles University in 1979, a turbulent year in which the leaders of Charter 77 (including Václav Havel) were sentenced to five years in prison. Embarking on a career in the science of minerals and geologic processes, Cílek also focused on the land, settlements, and long history of the inhabitation of Bohemia and Moravia, looking with the lens of an ethnographer as much as that of an earth scientist who saw far beyond the predicament and nightmares of recent and contemporary regimes. For the next decades he steadily surveyed a realm visible neither to the West, nor to most in his own country. Supporting himself modestly, teaching and working on scientific research and expeditions, he traveled abroad and through Central Europe, began to write popular books, and was the co-creator of a television series on Czech caves. Today he is well known and considered something of a Czech national treasure; his numerous prestigious prizes include the Tom Stoppard Prize for two of his books, *Krajiny vnitřní a vnější* (Inner and Outer Landscapes) and *Makom: Kniha míst* (Makom: Book of Places), and a prize from the Václav Havel Foundation, and he is a laureate of the Ministry of Ecology.

For residents of Western Europe and North America the Czech landscape lay behind the Iron Curtain for fifty years and was thought of distantly as Eastern Europe. Once the wall came down, Czechoslovakia, a nation cobbled together after World War I, could be seen as it truly was: the center of Europe. The phrase "Central Europe" returned and Prague once more was a European capital that looked both east and west, north and south. Bohemia is a place from which rivers flow north to the Elbe, the Oder, and the Baltic and south to the Danube, the Black Sea, and the Mediterranean.

The essays, tales, images, and experiences gathered here wander through a rich landscape, along back roads and into rarely visited and largely unknown towns and villages, hamlets and lonely hillsides, windswept plains, mines and caves. Cílek passes lightly over excavations he has made in caves inhabited by humans who hunted Pleistocene animals and, in turn, were hunted by long extinct carnivores. He seems almost familiar with later people, as they moved from Asia and the Caucasus, passing through with their herds, wheeled carts, horses, and bronze utensils, on their way as far west as Ireland and Spain. Whether one thinks of ancient troubles such as the Thirty Years' War or the more recent horrific slaughter of the Nazi era, Bohemia, Moravia, and the surrounding region have been involved in Western history continuously since the glaciers retreated to leave the stones and boulders Cílek frequently evokes. Long a granary of the Hapsburg Empire, the villages and towns of this lovely region have experienced an extraordinary amount of suffering, from the burning of Jan Hus at the stake and the brutal suppression of his followers to the slaughter of more than 33,000 Austrian and Russian troops in one day by Napoleon at the Battle of Austerlitz. Cílek and his colleagues witnessed the passage of German and Russian armies in their childhood, and with their students lived through the more recent crushing of the Prague Spring by tanks and long gray decades of Communist rule, outlasting and outmaneuvering their oppressors.

No wonder, then, that his writing takes a long view of things. He remarks that the Czech outlook—and his, we suppose—on neighboring Slovakia is one of a more ancient, primitive, romantic, and folkloric place, still inhabited by primitive souls close to the world of spirits and gods that has been lost in Bohemia and the cities. He writes, "It's sort of hard to explain contact with aspects of life—forests, rocks, and subterranean streams, but also folktales that bring one into an archaic but still living world of legends and rural sorcery." This, however, is precisely one of the things that he does in his peregrinations about the landscape and history of the region. At a time when global economics and consumer-driven industries seem to be homogenizing so much of the culture of nations and people on all continents, Cílek has embarked on a rescue mission, attempting to find and record aspects of life from an earlier era, one that was deeply rooted in place, with a sweep that includes obscure stones, ancient agriculture, local legends, and modern forensics. We expect such sensibilities from artists like the great Polish poet Czesław Miłosz, whose work is steeped in the soil and detailed history (anguish as well) of the people of the region north of Bohemia, or of earlier ethnographers such as Claude Lévi-Strauss in the jungles of Brazil trying to record the genius of a people and a vanishing way of life. It is unusual today to find a natural scientist who writes so eloquently about what he has seen and heard, thought and learned about his ancestral cultural fabric, and is so aware and sensitive to relationships that are invisible to most. Cílek is able to articulate a phenomenon that has been described by others as a process of departure from this realm of a spirit world that once included elves and the gods of the ancients.

෫

When we say that writing, or painting, or photography is poetic, what do we mean? Clearly such works are not what is commonly called poetry. Rather, we mean that a work exhibits a sensibility that partakes of concise vision and heightened perception. Often revelatory of aspects of life and their impact on our senses, imagination, and feelings, it may be tragic, passionate, dreamy, whimsical, or terrifying in the truths sensed and divulged. Just as poetic verse is charged and more potent than ordinary speech or narrative, whether quiet or loud, subtle or dramatic, it is sufficiently evocative to strike us as genuine, whether familiar or not. It speaks of the nature of things. The work in this volume is poetic in all of these senses.

A great amount has been said regarding the hazards, difficulties, and shortcomings of translation, especially regarding poetry and great literature. The concern is almost always over a perceived loss of sensibility and character, of whether the voice of an author or sympathy between diction and subject is adequately captured. As I do not read or write Czech, I can only see what has emerged into English, and it feels deeply insightful, robust, and straightforward, like the author himself. And yet there are phrases that open out into considerable spaces that allow speculation and distant views of other topics: "Over a longer time span, only the sediment of a smile, tranquility, and a certain weight remains of a proud and brutal history. How this is possible we don't know. When reminiscing about the past, we remember musicians and poets, but not bankers and police chiefs." Even artists may have a sense of melancholy, or frustration, that something has been lost between their ambitions and their work, that a gulf exists between a subject and its subsequent representation. They may perceive a gap, at times an enormous one, between the seeing, feeling, writing, drawing, or photographing. This dilemma haunts reflective artists of all sorts.

And yet, what we do have, what has been magically captured and expressed, is remarkable. In the case of superior artists it is to be treasured. For Václav Cílek, the result of his efforts to share his perceptions, insights, feelings, and flights of association, understandings, knowledge, whimsy, imagination, mistakes, conclusions, pronouncements, memories, and dreams of landscapes is worthy of celebration. While writing in the twentieth and twenty-first centuries, Cílek shifts from era to era, through geologic time, from the Middle Ages to today. Ruminations from Bronze Age Celtic events and scenes alternate with sly pronouncements regarding tragic bumblers of our own epoch, and move from human to animal to vegetable and back, challenging the reader, most likely a postmodern urban dweller, to think with him from within a tree or a stone or small creature. The world he conjures in these essays ranges widely, but most frequently evokes places and things once common in profound ways to people on all continents—mud and dust, clouds of insects, flocks of wild creatures, birds and herds, sunlight, small sounds, myths and darkness, stars and spirits, long walks through fields from town to town on foot in various weather.

For a number of years I took graduate students from the University of Pennsylvania to a handsome village in formerly German-speaking southern Bohemia where we studied the landscape and architecture. This was home to the people that figure prominently in these essays, the rich farmland studded with Jewish villages and farms that Hitler called the Sudetenland and annexed in 1938 as a prelude to invading the rest of the country a few years later. Across the border in Austria are medieval farm layouts along with a visually stunning patchwork of long narrow plow strips beautifully planted. On the Czech side, one finds a more barren, broad, open landscape. The depleted soil and ecological devastation wrought on large portions of the region by sixty years of bad government and ideological economic policy are stunning. Yet my students were enthralled to discover that a large number of people, old and young, prowled the countryside in all seasons on foot and by bicycle in summer and on skis in winter, and that "tramping," along with drinking and singing around campfires in the woods and fields, as well as mushroom hunting wherever one pleased, were considered socially acceptable and a traditional thing to do. Cílek's perambulations are a direct extension of this ingrained cultural tradition that grows from the place.

Today, as more and more of the earth's population leaves the countryside to dwell within ever-expanding regional cities, this is about to become a lost world. The larger subject under examination in Cílek's work is the transitory nature of landscapes and the destruction of one followed by the creation of another. In "Walking Through a Landscape" he writes:

> Walking through a landscape we experience a calm unlike
> the city, an indefinite sanctity in its configuration, a depth
> of time in its geological layers, and a sense that this earth was
> touched by generations of our ancestors and that some part
> of them has been absorbed into the earth and that some part
> of the earth has been absorbed into us. . . . We sometimes
> feel grief over the landscape we are losing under a network of
> highways, suburban developments, and industrial warehouses
> full of things that in the end we do not need.

As this landscape is altered or disappears, images of what it looked like become as precious as narratives such as Cílek's. Morna Livingston is a photographer, writer, and design teacher who, like Cílek, is particularly attuned to the relationship between people and the land. Also widely traveled and insightful about ecological history, she is observant of the beauty to be found in the quotidian much in a manner that one associates with poets. Livingston's work is quiet and deserving of close study. Over the past decade, in addition to teaching in Philadelphia, Livingston has spent considerable time in the Czech Republic, especially in the countryside and villages of Bohemia as well as Prague. Following an introduction to Anna Farova, the individual most responsible for discovering, exhibiting, and publishing Czech photographers in the West, Livingston has become a student of the visual as well as physical heritage of the region and nation. After the Velvet Revolution Farova produced a series of definitive volumes on the major Czech photographers of the twentieth century. Examining this work one can see that Morna Livingston's photographs, twenty-four of which are reproduced here, form a knowing extension of this realm of Czech photography—no small feat.

We expect great photographers to have a highly refined eye, to be masters of light, texture, tone, and composition. All of this we find in Livingston's photographs. We also expect photographers to see clearly, better than ourselves, and to search out significant experience and bring it back to us in the form of memorable images. At times these insights are valuable because they present common things that were right in front of us all the time. At other times they are truly new and strange, a revelation. This too, along with a serenity and calm that are rare in urban life for many today, we find in the photographs Livingston has made in the Czech Republic. The identification of many of her images implies as much: Apple trees on an old road in Písečné; Carp pond in Dačice; Ceiling reflected in holy water font; Pasture near Snake Hill; Cubist stair, House of the Black Madonna; and Moss-covered rock.

In an era drowning in images even before children began taking countless pictures with their cell phones, it is as difficult for people to slow down and carefully look at and think about a truly superb photograph as it is for them to listen to a great piece of music. In galleries, many people often spend more time reading labels on the wall than they do actually looking at the paintings or photographs. I strongly recommend that readers of this book spend as much time looking at each of the photographs as they do reading a couple of pages. The photographs are not illustrations of Cílek's text or anything else. Each photograph in its own way is an essay in much the same way that each of Cílek's narratives is—at times a clear, brief one, and at other times a more complex, slowly unfolding one. As with the written text, there is a gradual layering and additive effect. Both scientist-author and photographer wander about the landscape, through fields and woods, along streams, and into villages. Both notice things out of the corner of the eye that others often miss, places that are out of the way, or are quiet, almost to the point of being subversive—but not submissive. In Livingston's photographs one finds the qualities confronted in Cílek's essays—timelessness, strength, and beauty. These attributes are not commonly achievable through willful effort or design, but more often derive from natural and cultural processes, from an accumulation of use and cultivation, from layering and regeneration, stewardship and accident. At one point Cílek writes about vision remarking that if it is "true, it is usually a truth behind an image, rather than the truth of an image."

Two decades ago the landscape historian Catherine Howett remarked that "scholars in many disciplines, but especially philosophy, psychology, and cultural geography, have in recent years contributed to a growing body of literature analyzing the nature of human place experience . . . [all] concerned with helping us ultimately to understand better the dynamics of the myriad different kinds of relationships we humans have with the environments we shape and that shape us, including the natural world." In her essay "Systems, Signs, and Sensibilities" she singles out Yi-Fu Tuan and his groundbreaking study of what he termed "topophilia," "the effective bond between people and place or setting." Howett notes, "In a telling passage, Tuan explored the difference between the occasional native response to environment, unmediated by culturally imposed criteria, and the more distant, intellectualized experience that is especially common in advanced societies. A child, he observed, cares less for a composed picturesque view at the seashore than for the particular things and physical sensations he or she encounters there."

This collection of essays by Václav Cílek and photographs by Morna Livingston is a worthy addition to the Penn Studies in Landscape Architecture, for it presents both world perceptions—those of direct intuition and confrontation, reveling in the material richness of the earth and its creatures, along with a record of unmediated ancient fears and feelings, combined with the knowledge of two deeply informed, sophisticated intellectuals who happen to be serious artists. They see clearly, drawing on a superb memory, and are not beguiled by passing fashion or theory. This is a remarkable book, one that rescues a fragment of the world and offers us perception and knowledge of a very particular place, a cultural landscape of deep meaning, beauty, and value.

PREFACE

*Gathering Strength
and Drinking Dawn
in the Landscape
of Home*

*I will sit on a stump
by a forest spring
to gather strength
and drink dawn*
—Vítězslav Nezval*

We are returning from a vacation in Thailand or maybe the Canary Islands. It was beautiful, but had we stayed there a bit longer, we would soon have become bored. The painter Václav Rabas** used to say that it is important to find one's own square kilometer of landscape and try to understand it. Argentinean writer Jorge Luis Borges insisted that it is not as important to read books as it is to return to those books

---

* Vítězslav Nezval (1900–1958) was an important, prolific, and politically controversial poet whose early poems had a rare, playful beauty.

** Václav Rabas (1885–1954) was a landscape painter whose artistic focus for several decades was a small agricultural area near Krušovice, a village to the west of Prague.

🙌 *Apple trees on an old road in Písečné*

that one has already read. We contemplate landscapes and distinguish between them: "That one is beautiful, but this one is mine." Home is where we return to, and we leave it only so that we may return. And then it makes no difference whether we live below the monumental Pravčice Gate* or next to a barely mature spruce forest.

We spend only brief amounts of time in foreign countries, but in the landscapes of our home we grow old with the earth and the trees. Years later we return to the same places, pile up memories, and become rooted in the landscape. Hardly anyone can feel at home in more than two or three landscapes. A trip means rapture, excitement, and experience. The landscape of our home is a flux in which our spiritual and natural sides mingle and the resulting blend is poised—like music or poetry—somewhere between humans and the elements.

Certain nations and civilizations like to travel because they believe beauty and truth must be somewhere else, since they cannot find them at home. Other nations or groups feel it is quite sufficient to understand their own piece of the earth. This is the difference between people from northern and southern Italy, between Germans and Austrians, and between the French on the Atlantic coast and their compatriots on the Mediterranean. What can the world possibly offer a vintner from Pálava or Hodonín,** when he has all the strength of the earth and sun right in his wine cellar?

We Bohemians and Moravians are both. Influenced by the restless Germans and especially the Saxons with their proclivity for hiking, we set off for foreign lands, but we are truly comfortable only where we can drop into a familiar pub or go mushroom picking. Simply at home—where we are not afraid of the forest, where we can't get lost for very long, and where we can find our way to the station even from the deepest wilderness. We are very lucky to be living in

---

* The Pravčice Gate is a large sandstone arch in the so called Saxon-Bohemian Switzerland region which was visited frequently by the first Continental Romantics.
** Pálava and Hodonín are sunny and dry regions in southern Moravia well known for wine production.

this country, where everything is small yet immensely diverse. I have written this many times, but I must repeat it: to get to know this country is a lifelong endeavor. Bohemia and Moravia* form a landscape for connoisseurs and wayfarers, which, rather than tantalizing us with grandiose exaltation, propagates refined strength and a faintly melancholic calm. The cliffs are small here, the colors muted, the rivers are not turbid waterways, and the waterfalls resemble children's toys rather than places where roaring waters careen into deep chasms.

This landscape is so mild and yet so rich that we do not even realize how lucky we are to be walking through it. It doesn't dazzle; it replenishes. We don't even think about it anymore; we just put on our shoes and pack a bottle of water, a map, a notepad, and maybe a camera or a few pages copied from this book, and we set off for places where the earth is still strong and strengthens us as well.

* Bohemia is the central region of the Czech Republic, and Moravia forms the country's eastern part. The name Bohemia is mentioned by Strabo and other writers of antiquity as the land of the Boii, a Celtic tribe, hence Boiohaemum, later Bohemia. The adjective *bohemian* originated much later, when French and Spanish armies returning from medieval Bohemia attracted Roma, or Gypsies, whom they mistakenly called Bohemians. Still later, people who lived freely, unconventionally and outside the social establishment—in particular avant-garde artists—called themselves bohemians.

Geodiversity comprises a whole range of landscape
features, including geological, geomorphological,
paleontological, soil, hydrological and atmospheric
features, systems and processes.
—Australian Natural Heritage Charter, 1997

Introduction: Definition of the Term

The term *geodiversity* was probably first used by Vojen Ložek
in conversations about the natural sciences without any later written elaboration on the concept. The discussion centered on the fact
that there exist whole monographs on biodiversity, while the term
geodiversity is hardly used. I found it only recently in the Australian
Natural Heritage Charter, quoted above. Geodiversity is the basis of
a substantial part of biodiversity, and functions as a "superstructural"
phenomenon. There are an inexhaustible number of cases where geological and geomorphological characteristics determine vegetation
type—from rocky steppes to riparian forests and valley phenomena.
The two—the biological and the geological—are so closely connected
that while we perceive them as a natural unit, only seldom do we view

such a naturalistic whole solely from the point of view of earth sciences. The aim of this essay is to draw attention to the necessity of targeted protection of geodiversity, about which until recently the view prevailed, more or less automatically, that it—unlike plants and animals—is able to protect itself.

When making a list of protected and other significant geological localities for the Ministry of the Environment, I was thinking about geodiversity as one of the basic categories of protection for the non-living environment. Definitionally, I consider it to be the substrative and morphological diversity of a certain territory. The Australian definition is more detailed, encompassing a territory's hydrological and microclimatic conditions as well, and taking into account the possible existence of valuable paleontological sites. In addition, it contains the presupposition that geodiversity is subject to natural processes of transformation. In existing works on environmental protection, the concept of geodiversity is more or less subsumed within a range of other, often difficult-to-define terms such as a *habitat* or *landscape*. In the past several years, geological aspects of environmental protection have received increasing attention—for example, in the creation of geological parks. It is my belief that geodiversity may, or rather must, become one of the basic concepts of environmental and landscape protection.

The Story of a Trench for a Telephone Cable

As a result of gas lines and underground telephone cables laid over the past several years, dozens of kilometers of trenches reaching down to the bedrock have been excavated, which enables us to examine what the original geodiversity of the landscape was like and when it was depleted. Evidence of this comes in the form of fragments of slag, brick, and prehistoric or modern glazed shards. In recent years

I have systematically walked along a number of trenches dug in the Czech Karst.* Let us now set off along a Czech Telecom trench running from the Karlštejn railway station in the direction of Liteň and have a look at what has happened to the landscape.

The trench first runs from the railway station across a wide floodplain to the walls of the valley. The profile consists of brown flood clays located as high as five to six meters above the current level of the Berounka River. The brown-glazed shards of earthenware demonstrate that floodwaters reached this height during the past 150 to 200 years. There can be only one reason for the occasional stones that appear in the otherwise fine-grained clays—they were brought here by melting glaciers. And when we gaze across the valley and imagine a line six meters above the current level of the river's surface, we see that in the event of another great flood at least several hundred—but probably several thousand—cabins and houses would lie within this flooded area.

The trench now leaves the floodplain and climbs up the hillside—we discover the remains of terraced fields and orchards here. There used to be many more small ravines on the slope; today they are clogged with earth and fragments of quite modern bricks (at most one hundred years old) that lie as deep as 1.5 meters. In other places it is evident that diabase rocks once penetrated the surface but were broken off—probably by the eighteenth and nineteenth centuries—so as not to obstruct agriculture. Today the slope of the valley is smooth and relatively featureless, but until recently it was furrowed with small gorges and accentuated with low rocks.

The trench gradually climbs up to a plateau along a golf course. Here, by contrast, a sort of cockpit relief of small hills and depressions was created on the remains of the agricultural terraces. (The nature

* The Czech Karst is the limestone area between Prague and Beroun, and is well known for its almost six hundred caves, numerous archaeological sites, and rich plant and animal life.

conservation body and those of us who have been advising it recently did not mind the golf course, but we did not know that such a course requires a specific type of lawn in which the local grass vegetation must be "smothered" somewhat.) The trench now continues on for a kilometer through flat agricultural land, where there is seemingly nothing that it could harm. But right behind the golf course we come across a buried moor with thick black soil that contains the reddish stalks of ancient reeds. A little bit farther on not only is there another wetland, but suddenly a rocky wall of contact metamorphic Liteň shale rises to the surface. Today there is a desert of corn here, but only recently this monolithic area—the pride of every agricultural cooperative—was a system of several fields separated by strips of uncultivated land that lay on the natural fractures of the topography. Between the fields there were two spring basins and at least one sludgy lake. We sense newts, globeflowers, and orchids here, and maybe even ducks nested here as they do in the wetland above Tetín* that still exists today.

A similar picture can be seen farther on, closer to Liteň—the trench shows other strips of uncultivated land, a rocky outcropping, a small spring, and several houses situated much closer to the road than modern apartment buildings. The overall impression: where only recently a range of habitats existed alongside one another, in a landscape with high geo- and thus also biodiversity, there are today three segments of landscape—one large field down on the floodplain, one leveled slope, and another field on the plateau. And a similar story is told by a trench running from Beroun to Tobolka and on to Brdy, and by many other probes scattered throughout Bohemia. The insensitive use of landscape has certainly contributed its share, but we can also observe something else—something that comes from the psychology of humankind. I would call it a "linearizing and leveling impulse" that

---

* Tetín is a village in the Czech Karst located on a large prehistoric settlement, a pilgrimage site where St. Ludmila, the grandmother of St. Václav (Wenceslaus), was murdered.

drives us to level slopes and straighten riverbeds—to remove even that natural chaos which is productive. I once saw the owner of a summer cabin drag a heating stove two kilometers into the forest to block the mouth of a medieval adit. I think he did it out of some archaic inspiration to close an entrance to the underworld.

The Loss of Geodiversity

The literature of rural realism of the late nineteenth and early twentieth centuries (the works of Karel Václav Rais, Josef Holeček, Karolina Světlá, and others) repeatedly mentions the removal of stones from the fields, the smoothing and filling of erosion furrows, the consolidation of small fields into larger units, the laborious slicing off of pastures and their conversion into arable land. Topsoil from the valleys was even brought to fields in the foothills. Heaps of stones from the fields of the Bohemian-Moravian Highlands and Central Bohemian Uplands, stone walls in southern Bohemia, overgrown terraced fields in the Kokořín area* all bear witness to a centuries-long struggle for soil. This cultivation of the land was accompanied by the removal of small natural formations such as protruding rocks, the draining of wetlands, and other losses of geodiversity. The terrain was very often segmented by strips of uncultivated land and differentiated by paths on slopes that often grew into deeply eroded furrows. The ravine in Zeměchy near Kralupy, for example—which is over fifteen meters deep—was likely created through the erosion of a farm track. Thus, mainly in hilly areas a new and usually quite picturesque broken topography emerged, made up of long strips of uncultivated land. In the flatlands, however, we can only expect a landscape with

---

* The Kokořín area, located north of Prague, features romantic sandstone canyons.

significantly diminished geodiversity as a result of large-scale, deliberate, and systematic work for centuries.

In some areas, mining of raw materials over many years has had a strong negative impact. Lime has been burned relatively intensively in the Czech Karst and many other places since the sixteenth century. Observations from Hungary (the Bükk Mountains) and Slovakia (the Zemplín Mountains and elsewhere) show that limestone mining and the production of quicklime involves first collecting loose lapies and then breaking off the naturally exposed occurrences. It is not possible to determine today how many loose limestone boulders, fields of lapies, and small rocks lay, for example, in the Czech Karst and other smaller places where limestone occurs, but originally the amount must have been incomparable to the present state. Upon closer examination we find that all reachable outcroppings, especially on the small limestone islands, have been broken off or destroyed.

Albert Vojtěch Velflík (1913–1917) mentions that "huge solitary boulders were once abundant in Bohemia, but now occur only rarely—especially granite ones, many of which fell victim to the construction of railways during the second half of the last century, used as temporary quarries for acquiring excellent building stone." He cites the example of a large, beautiful boulder called Baba near Kralovice, which was six meters high and which was broken apart in 1913 for building stone and taken to Plzeň on 110 railway wagons. Less conspicuous is the practice of collecting smaller stones used to build villages or stone walls. In view of the several thousand villages that have existed since roughly 1250, this amounts to huge displacements of stone material. In the total figure one must additionally include the mass of stone used for railways, river navigation, and various technical structures. There is some question as to whether we can even imagine how some Bohemian and Moravian landscapes looked before the "great collection of stones."

Today we do not even realize what an immense change our rivers have undergone. According to a preserved account of the marble altar in the Church of the Virgin Mary in Prague's Lesser Quarter, it was hewn from a great boulder pulled out of the Berounka River. If we take a walk today through the Berounka's limestone canyon, we will not come across a single large limestone block or protruding rock. Stones from the Vltava River were being removed at least as early as 1547, when a decree on the matter was issued by Emperor Ferdinand I in an effort to support commerce. Some time after 1640, the Strahov abbot Kryšpín Fuka invited military engineers to make the Vltava navigable. He had the rocks rising out of the water blasted, for example, near Zbraslav, although only after 1729 did such efforts finally succeed in crushing the rocks and making the river navigable as far as Kamýk. Nearly five hundred years of river modifications have transformed many European rivers from picturesquely dangerous elements to innocuous muddy channels. If we consider the original state of the Vltava above Prague, we can find a suitable analogy in the central Sázava River, which—although significantly smaller—has occasional crags, protruding boulders, and gravel bars. In this connection the Thaya Canyon in the Podyjí National Park presents an interesting case—while today it looks almost untouched, in the late Middle Ages and early modern era it was a landscape influenced more by people than is true now.

The entire central portion of the Bohemian Labe (Elbe in other languages) and many other rivers were rid of their systems of several generations of blind river branches. The idea that places like Pardubice or Most were accessible only by long fascine bridges leading through wetlands and still pools is quite fanciful today. Also gone are the once so numerous river islands, and dozens of spring basins and wetlands have disappeared from agricultural land.

The North Bohemian Brown Coal Basin is considered one of the most damaged landscapes in the world. If we look at it from the point of view of the next fifty years, however, north Bohemia may become an important tourist region combining the mountain and forest landscapes of the Ore Mountains with extensive bodies of water filling former open-pit mines. The lignite will have been extracted by then, the environment will be cleaner in general, and a significant portion of the landscape will be free of human settlement. If we recultivate the landscape correctly today, it may one day be said of us: "They destroyed one beautiful landscape, but created another one in its place."

From the point of view of the twentieth century, the central Bohemian Labe has probably fared worst of all. Until the last third of the nineteenth century it was a broad valley with numerous still meanders, pools, riparian meadows, and forests, which were separated from the fields by a large inundated area. An appetite for farmland, regulation of the Labe, the proximity of large industrial centers, and waterway and mainly railway transport changed this territory into a densely built up industrialized zone with the Labe as its central channel. Before World War II, up to thirty-five thousand people used to come to a system of river beaches—Grado—in Čelákovice* on the weekends. Today, the whole central Bohemian Labe is a recreational dead zone. Its prospects over the next fifty years are less favorable than those of the North Bohemian Brown Coal Basin. The whole region has been affected—to a certain extent irreversibly (it is not possible to restore the meanders or reclaim the built-up area)—by unrestrained development and an inability to plan further than a few years into the future. A similar story is unfolding in the suburban zones around Prague and other cities, where prefabricated housing developments will begin to decay in about fifty years.

---

* Čelákovice is a small town to the east of Prague on the Labe River which is known for vampire burials. Archaeological research discovered a small burial site there dating from the tenth and eleventh centuries where corpses had been pierced with wooden stakes to prevent them from rising up from the grave.

For us—in contrast to the Gothic aristocrat or the baroque magnate—it is difficult to plan fifty to one hundred years ahead, but certain guidelines can be drawn from the principles of permanent sustainability and emphasis on protection of water, soil, and landscape space. In other words, one cannot stop the earth, and in view of the possibility of climatic and social change it is suitable to remember a back door—the reserves that the landscape can provide.

Creating Geodiversity

In European and American civilization some twenty tons of rock and soil per person per year are displaced. These are mainly building materials, motorway embankments, bedrock, limestone, asphalt, and other raw materials. On the one hand, geodiversity is being destroyed, but on the other it is also being created. The extent to which new geodiversity is desirable depends on whether it significantly changes the character of a landscape or, rather, it accentuates and enhances its natural features. Many, especially small, irregular quarries enrich a landscape, while a linear motorway embankment suppresses its character. In general, it is desirable to create smaller bodies of water and rocky outcroppings (i.e., precisely those elements that have gradually disappeared during the last several centuries), while more significant changes are problematic and must be evaluated individually for each specific case and landscape. Consequently, environmental protection throughout Europe faces a challenge that involves not only protecting the disappearing original natural environment but also actively managing a new anthropogenic environment, which is heading toward a certain target state—for example, the combination of a natural oak forest and geological profiling in a deeply recessed motorway.

The Temporal Dimension of Changes

Changes in the nesting of birds, the quality of meadow vegetation, the state of forests, and similar phenomena are evident over a span of several years. The forested, deforested, and reforested Šumava Mountains* could all be experienced within one generation. We usually feel a need to protect that which is changing before our eyes. Analogous to the incomparably slower progress of geological time than biological time, changes in geodiversity have been inconspicuous over the centuries, but in their entirety resulted in a complete change in the character of the landscape. This is why I believe we must carefully consider any modifications we make in the landscape—it is technically easy to destroy a rock formation obstructing a planned road, but we should bear in mind that several similar formations have already been destroyed in a given area that will never be returned to their place. The landscape is being depleted stone by stone.

Microclimatic Diversity

The Australian definition of geodiversity also includes climatic and microclimatic conditions. Especially in times of global climatic change, it is difficult to protect or preserve microclimatic diversity in practice. Nevertheless, there are examples of systems that are extremely sensitive to microclimatic changes.

Case one—frozen scree slopes: This is a group of about twenty-five scree fields that are frozen or deeply chilled until late spring or summer. Glacial relicts, especially spiders and beetles, have been preserved here. It is a unique phenomenon in central Europe—for exam-

---

* Šumava, also known as the Bohemian Forest, is the Gabreta Forest first mentioned by geographers of antiquity. Today it is a national park where wilderness in nature has evoked a wilderness in human hearts.

ple, it has not been recorded on the territory of the significantly larger Germany. The preservation of scree slope ecosystems is directly dependent on the right speed of cold airflow. If I dig a geological probe or an insect trap in the lower part of a scree slope, I could change the airflow and destroy the system.

Case two—cave environments: The speed of a dripstone's growth depends on the level of carbon dioxide saturation in the precipitating solutions. If I remove the topsoil from the space above a cave or make large-scale changes to vegetation, for example, deforestation, I will change the speed of water seepage. This could allow rainwater to easily penetrate into the cave; here it would become saturated with carbon dioxide and corrode the dripstones rather than augment them. In both cases, maintaining the right microclimatic system is an essential condition for preserving the environment.

Case three—riparian forests: The stability of these splendid ecosystems depends to a large extent on annual flooding, the creation of new point bars, fresh-cut banks, slipping banks, and pools full of water after spring. Build a levee and you will harm nature.

The Leveling, Draining, and Linearizing Impulse

Many problems surrounding the preservation of monuments, forests, and the environment in general have a psychological basis. The destruction of villages and ill-conceived urban development in the postwar era came about in part because of views held by the first party functionaries who, in many cases, came from picturesque—yet at that time also poverty-stricken—cottages and historical houses that they hated and endeavored to replace with something else. The often disastrous result in the form of decaying prefabricated tenements on the outskirts of villages is well known. Urbanism, architecture, and the use of landscape in the twentieth century are permeated by a sort of primitive neofunctionalism that loves right-angled waterways, large level fields, flat roofs, and simple yet often inhuman geometric shapes. When in 1929 Le Corbusier outlined the city of tomorrow, he wrote: "A flat area is an ideal place for a contemporary city. Everywhere that traffic becomes overcrowded, a flat area offers the possibility of resolving this problem in a normal way. A river should flow far from the city. It is a sort of fluid railway, freight yard, and transloading point. In a decent house a staircase for servants does not lead through the drawing room—even if the servant is charming or if the view of boats is pleasing to the eye of the pedestrian leaning over the railing." In this view, the ideal district of the future Prague would be Jižní Město.* A late product of this type of thinking is geometric and self-replicating suburbia. In most cases, however, today's contemporary living space is characterized by a return to complex, irregular shapes with numerous social and natural spaces.

This can be easily observed in historical city centers (the opening of courtyards, the renovation of labyrinths), revitalization projects, and the reconstruction of gardens. The times are again returning to the view that irregularity is welcome and that the geometrization of a landscape means its depletion. Most natural scientists have a natural perception of landscape, but many technicians are subject to "engineering aesthetics," according to which, for example, a landscape with a motorway can be aesthetically superior to a landscape without a motorway, or a straightened river is "more civilized" than a meandering one. Most existing engineered modifications to landscape have been carried out in the spirit of Le Corbusier, in the view that the best landscape for humans is a flat, homogeneous area that can be dominated and where all geodiversity is suppressed.

---

* Jižní Město is a large Communist-era condominium project located in the southern part of Prague.

Landscape as a Storage Space
for Semifunctional Things

The television documentary series *In Search of Lost Time* by Karel Čáslavský and Pavel Vantuch examined the construction of the railway line from Vsetín to Bylnice in eastern Moravia. In regard to landscape, it was very important evidence of the transformation of the usual, rather unphotogenic scenery in the close proximity of a railway. Since the flysch* here is very prone to sliding, it was necessary during the construction to dig extensive trenches and perform earthmoving work. These modifications seemed quite aggressive at the time, but today the railway fits in well with the surrounding landscape. Much more interesting, however, was a comparison of the state of the railway station and its vicinity then and now. The original buildings are still being used, but they look worse than in 1918. This is due mainly to a large number of various additions, including sheds and storage space for equipment and machines, that "may come in handy some day."

It is inconceivable today that a person of average wealth would put all of his or her property into a single trunk or cabinet, as was still common before World War II. In the same way that our homes have filled with things and furniture, also our landscape has filled with various sheds, garages, and additions that generally contain semifunctional junk. And the story is similar for automobiles—not only do they pollute the air, they also take up the space of people and trees. The main thing we need is a change from the consumption model of behavior to one of a society that needs fewer things, hence consumes less energy and consequently produces less garbage. In the meantime, however, we can respond by further developing public transportation and by

* Flysch is a geological term for tertiary sediments where rhythmic layers of slates and claystones enhance runoff and initiate frequent landslides.

regulating automobile traffic. In the coming century, large cities will experience various crises, the solutions to which will cost billions—for example, building long-distance water pipelines, motorway bypasses, and the like. It is easier, however, to invest in a dignified and attractive life in the country and, in so doing, to avoid the problems of urban life. We can also help cities by taking care of the village.

Adopt a Highway!

In the globalized world, the environment is globalized, too. In early September 2000 the large international conference "Natura megapolis"—Nature Conservation in Big Cities—was held at Prague's Municipal House. One of the conference's main topics was "urban ecology" and its future. It was basically about how to ensure the dignified coexistence of automobiles, people, and nature. Soon, some 70 percent of the world's population will be living in cities, and human settlements will account for some 12–15 percent of the earth's surface. At the same time, however, islands of disturbed yet valuable nature survive in urban agglomerations. In Prague we can observe 2,000 plant species (compared to only 1,300 in Rome, which is three times larger), 126 bird species, 120 inconspicuous species of small mollusks, and 400 species of spiders. Prague but also Bratislava or Valencia are hidden natural reserves. This is not a matter of course—in the center of Amsterdam we can find fewer than 200 species of plants, and in Japanese cities the situation is even worse. In Osaka, which was built two thousand years ago in the marshes of the Yodo River, there were a mere hundred thousand trees until the 1960s; today, however, there are half a million, and with them the birds and butterflies have been returning as well. In the context of the diversity of living nature, Prague is our most valuable nature preserve!

The problem with such urban islands lies not in a decrease in the number of species—this figure has not changed much in Prague since the 1930s, and may even have risen slightly. No significant extinction or depletion is occurring in European natural environments or even in cities, but something more fundamental is happening. Most significantly, nature has fragmented into small units. In place of a large and therefore stable forest, we find a small woodland, a dump, a warehouse, and then another small woodland. The abundance of species living in such a landscape is the same or even greater than in a single large forest, but the system is more vulnerable. It is more difficult for the system to cope with changes and it also loses its influence on the surrounding environment—it can no longer absorb dust particles or precipitation. As civilization has become more vulnerable to climatic variation and, for example, oil shocks, nature too is becoming more vulnerable. This does not mean imminent catastrophe; rather, it is an indication that we are increasingly shifting toward some hard-to-determine threshold of equilibrium, beyond which lies first natural and social chaos, and then some new (probably less favorable) equilibrium.

Another very problematic process is the globalization of nature. Analogous to the expansion throughout society of one dominant culture, whose emblems are the proverbial McDonald's hamburgers, nature too is becoming more and more homogeneous. A full third of Prague's two thousand embryophytes are of foreign origin. They are "economic refugees" from Sakhalin, the Far East, Ukraine, and the United States, who came here more or less by chance and found suitable living conditions. One of the most common woody plants in the central parts of Prague is the ailanthus, which comes from the Far East and has spread here thanks to the fact that it does not mind the polluted and salty urban environment. Similarly, it has been a matter of great concern among Japanese natural scientists that mainly European and American species have been spreading in the garbage-filled estuary on which the Tokyo Bay district was built. There have been vociferous discussions in Chicago on whether to cut down invasive European wood plants, especially buckthorn, which are disrupting local habitats. Natural scientists are thus discussing the same issue as politicians and protectors of national cultures: what to do about immigrants who threaten the traditional values of the original population?

A general answer offers itself along the following lines: it is necessary to maintain sufficiently broad and therefore stable areas with the original culture. I use the word culture here intentionally, in a general sense that comprises both a forest ecosystem and, for example, a tradition of puppet theater. Furthermore, it is also necessary to regulate immigration, but since this is unfeasible technically, we come to the last, and, from the point of view of the majority society, the main phase—learning to live with the Vietnamese shopkeeper, the ailanthus from the Far East, or the New Zealand family bungalow.

We can observe a great shift in the perception of urban nooks that until recently were scorned. Forest and soil have their economic function. A ranger today is not a forester, but a wood producer. What is left for nature are either reserves or areas where trees can grow but that are not forests with woodcutters—cemeteries, mounds, old quarries and sandpits, unused space.

In London, for example, the railway maintains eight hundred kilometers of embankments. For many urban residents, a daily train ride is their only contact with nature. Moreover, embankments work as important biocorridors—the only routes along which nature can expand in an otherwise built-up environment. Some of the embankments are now intentionally maintained as long, narrow islands of nature. London Wildlife Trust has even published an informational guide for train passengers about the plants, birds, and animals that live on the embankments and that can be observed on this very civil safari. Similar care is devoted to urban parks and river banks. It is also necessary for educational reasons—city children lacking direct contact with nature will fail to understand why it is necessary to protect it, and will also be deprived of experiencing it. In Chicago a movement called "Adopt a highway!" was founded that aims to encourage communities to maintain the naturally rich and aesthetically impressive, "garden-like" motorway embankments as one of only a few places where it is possible to develop urban nature in a creative manner.

The greatest enemy of urban nature is a selfish approach to urban planning and the viciously asserted economic superiority of wealthy investors. We could find many examples in the Czech Republic, but let us cite one in Jerusalem, where Ruth Enis from the Israel Institute of Technology counted a total of nine city plans between 1918 and 1968. All of them respected the spiritual traditions of this extraordinary city. They took into account that the spirituality of this city was closely connected with how the city looked from a distance. One could see the significance of Jerusalem already from its panorama. It was basically a matter of building a zone of open areas and green space that would separate the Holy City from the growing suburbs. Instead, pressure from investors led to construction right up to the borders of the city's historic center. Urban planner Arthur Kutcher assessed this type of urban planning with words that have a broader meaning: "The essential, generally shared awareness that the spiritual essence of Jerusalem is inseparably connected with its visual value is being ignored today; in fact it is not even being considered. Instead, a new view of Jerusalem is being implemented today—it is a source of income that must be exploited. Its spiritual and visual value are commodities that must be sold."*

* The suburbanization of the Holy Land is changing it completely, wiping away the landscapes of the Old and New Testaments. What was once the loss of Jerusalem's character is rapidly becoming the loss of the genius loci of large areas of the Holy Land.

Protecting Geodiversity

Existing preservation practice has usually treated geological bedrock as something that is mainly part of the vegetation rather than the animal realm, and not as something on which direct emphasis needs to be placed. However, a broader view based on historical analysis shows that geodiversity—like biodiversity—is affected by change, is gradually depleted, but can also be created anew. It works on a different time scale and takes place in a great number of sizes. It is necessary to distinguish it as a separate, albeit connected, category of environmental protection that is gradually emancipating itself from that of the better-known biodiversity. In Europe this process is evident, for example, in the creation of geological parks.

In a particular landscape it is then necessary to realize that not only geological outcroppings but also the properties of the substrate, the elevation of a valley floor, the existence of loose stones, and other topographical features have value in and of themselves, that is, even if they do not form the habitat for certain valuable biological systems. In view of the huge transfers of material in construction and mining, the concept of geodiversity also has a targeted futurological function—to design modifications to terrain or topsoil so that they will one day form an interesting natural nook.

The Superiority of the Nineteenth Century

In some ways, the nineteenth century was superior to the twentieth as well as to the present one. It was a calmer period, people had more time, they were collected, and it was natural for them to speak Czech, German, and Latin. There were few scholars; they knew each other and exchanged their findings. They could devote years to a single topic. None of today's scholars will ever have such comprehensive knowledge of classical literature as the nineteenth-century grammar school student who was drilled from early childhood to memorize Tacitus and Horace. Today, no one can master Slavic poetry because people who can read Russian, Polish, and Serbian are no longer; in Karel Hynek Mácha's* time and later, however, this was common knowledge for an intellectual. And something similar applies to folklore, comparative mythology, and—as we would call it today—cultural anthropology.

When Primus Sobotka was writing his extensive monograph on flora in Slavic national songs and rituals (1879), he had the National Museum's library at his disposal, filled with folk literature collections that would be difficult to access today. He read in all Slavic languages,

---

* Karel Hynek Mácha (1810–1836) was a beloved Czech Romantic poet and is considered one of the most important Czech poets.

but, most important, in his time folklore still drew on living, archaic sources. The folklore of the nineteenth century was still driven by the inertia of form and disposition that it had acquired some time during the Bronze Age or from time immemorial generally. In the section that follows, I select, combine, and slightly abridge sentences from Sobotka's monumental monograph. I do not aspire to present a new interpretation here, but merely to understand his opinions, especially about trees.

The Influence of Plants on the Human Mind

What ineffable desire steals into your soul when you walk through a murmuring grove in a shaded valley, what dark terror seizes your heart when after a long time you find yourself in a tall forest beneath centuries-old giants, and how completely different you will feel on a wide steppe, where the fickle eye searches in vain for an object to rest upon. *This is how the special character of every landscape makes its imprint in the mind of the person who dwells there.* Those who live in the mountains are usually adventurous, while inhabitants of fertile lowlands are cheerful or even frivolous. In our country, too, one can observe the difference between a "highlander" and a "lowlander." Not just the supple character of the landscape but also the flora have a significant influence on the human mind. A light beech forest makes one cheerful, a mighty oak forest inspires decisiveness and determined action, while a dark spruce forest awakens longing and sorrowful memories in the soul.

In a garden of flowers, your everyday worries will vanish and the creases of anxiety will disappear from your forehead. Is it even possible to stroll with indifference through an orchard where the branches bend under the weight of ripening fruit? A Slav, says Ladislav Štúr, is connected to nature with an inseparable bond. He observes it constantly and finds within it the disposition of his soul.

Beech tree in Lysice

He takes natural phenomena as his own and in this connection they are like old friends; each understands the other even without expressive words.

When people used to consider all the objects around them to be animate beings, they naturally had to have regard for them. The mighty contours of trees filled them with reverence, and they heard the voice of the divine in the rustling leaves. The mysterious darkness filled them with a solemn terror. Perhaps even the Czech word *háj* ("grove") originally meant a protected place—guarded, as the dwelling of forest gods. We can still hear a remnant of those times in the Czech expression *zahájit schůzi* ("to commence a meeting"). Etymologically this meaning originates from a former practice of commencing a court of law by erecting barriers between judge and opposing parties—compare German *Gericht hegen*. In older usage the verb *zahájit* can mean "to enclose, to fence off." Important national deliberations and tribunals took place here; this is where the dead were laid to rest. It was forbidden to enter certain groves on pain of death. The trees served as counsels and witnesses.

Individual trees were also held in high regard, either because of their height or their location—above a spring or by a path. Even today, people hang pictures on such trees and come to pray next to them. Serbians believe that if you chop down such a tree you will die, but you can avert your fate by chopping off a hen's head on the stump with the same axe. In all such cases, the tree was considered the sanctuary or body of a strange deity.

The Tree as a Person

One does not need too big an imagination to see the similarity between a tree and a person. Branches are easily mistaken for arms and the pith of a tree is like the soul of a person (the black elder has a white soul, says Vladislav Zadrobílek).* Both human and plant come from a seed, grow slowly and mature, bloom, bear fruit, gradually wither, and die. Many trees, especially fruit trees, live about as long as people. Genealogy is also based on this analogy, in which the founder of a lineage is represented by the main root and his descendants by branches. There were times when people even ascribed intellect and emotion to trees. This was the case in particular for fruit trees, which were regarded as family members like a goat or a cow.

The best evidence of this sentiment comes from Christmas customs. A farmer used to invite trees to dinner. His wife would go from tree to tree, and with hands wet from dough she would call: "Tree, rejuvenate, rejuvenate!" A crass Polish farmer would take an axe in hand, go from tree to tree, tap on each one (especially on those that bore little fruit) and say: "Will you produce, or won't you produce?" Serbians go to their garden on St. Stephen's Day with an axe, drive it into a tree, and ask: "Will you bear fruit?" A second person then craftily responds for the tree: "I will!" It is the Slavic custom to try to induce trees to yield a harvest by threat or by flattery and bribery. In some places they throw apples at trees; in others they bury bits of food under them. The important thing is that they believe the tree can hear them, that they can communicate with it and somehow reach an agreement. On Good Friday before sunrise people in some Czech regions kneel down under a tree and say:

> I pray to you, green tree,
> that God may reward you!

And it is not clear whether the farmer is praying to the tree or on its behalf—possibly both. Fruit trees were informed of the death of the farmer in both Slavic and German cultures: "Der Wirt ist tot."

* Vladislav Zadrobílek (1932–2010) was a hermetic philosopher, poet, and one of the last Czech practical alchemists.

The forest is considered a sort of municipality, with its own rights. In former times, certain forests—like rivers and lakes—required human sacrifices. It was better for a village to give them a person of their own choosing than to let the forest choose. The woodcutter begs forgiveness of the tree that he is about to cut down. Ancient is the legend of trees that bleed when they are cut. Both grass and trees grieve when a calamity befalls the earth.

The Link Between Human and Plant Life

Humans not only consider the tree a being, they also believe in some mysterious bond between the two of them. Legend tells of a woman whose soul lived in a willow at night, and when her husband cut it down, the woman died as well. There is an old custom in many places of planting a tree when a baby is born. The tree then becomes a tree of life, a botanical guardian angel. In Switzerland, they plant apple trees for boys and pear trees for girls. Sometimes it came to pass that a father became angry with his undutiful son, took an axe, and cut down his tree. It also happens that people who leave their homeland leave behind a plant or tree, so that their friends can see how they are doing in the distant land. A Cossack enlisting in the army tells his lover to watch his maple tree; if it bows its green crown, this will mean that he is dead.

Who knows why that strange custom of the Christmas tree took root so easily here? It may be connected to the wedding tree, where gilded ornaments, pine cones as symbols of fertility, and various bounties were hung. The bride had to shake the tree and watch whether a toy in the form of a cradle or a doll fell down. Also the maypole is a tree of life. The connection with flora persists even after death, and this is why people sometimes plant flowers or bushes on graves, believing that the soul of the dead will return to the flower, as we remember well from Karel Václav Erben's poem "Wild Thyme." On the graves of the innocent who were executed, plants grow whose shape or color point to the crime. Elsewhere, reed pipes or a violin made from the wood of a tree where someone was killed play very strange songs. This is why it is not advisable to pick flowers at a cemetery, lest the dead come for them.

People Transform into Plants

They do it either out of grief or to escape shame. The cowwheat is called "Ivan and Maria" in Little Russia after a brother and sister who were turned into it, as they had lived unknowingly in a forbidden covenant. Girls who waited in vain for their lovers turned into chicory and white poplar. A proud stepmother would turn into a pansy, a Cossack into a thorn, and his lover into a water elder. When a mother cursed her son, he sat on a horse and turned into a maple tree. Buckwheat is a princess abducted by the Tatars.

Forest Gods, Illnesses, and Prophecies

Václav Krolmus* noted a case of a white woman emerging from a linden tree in a bright glare. In a Serbian song, there is a pine tree on which a young girl, shining like the sun, comes to sit. When the tree dies, the girl vanishes as well. Certain forest creatures such as fairies are also water creatures. It is not advisable to mingle the world of people

* Václav Krolmus (1790–1861) was a Catholic priest, Czech patriot, and amateur archaeologist who specialized in "pagan histories" and sacred places.

with that of lesser gods. The goddess of all summer flora is sometimes called Bába.* Sorcerers sometimes write their dark messages on tree leaves or in apples. Sometimes they pass ailments on to a tree or bush by tearing off a strip of the ailing one's clothing and hanging it on a branch. Whoever removes the cloth will contract the ailment. Similarly, there are trees into which nails or pegs are hammered to relieve a toothache in the belief that the pain itself will be pounded in as well.

Maybe the Slavs, too, like the Greeks, prophesied from the murmur of sacred oaks. In other places, not just apples but also oak apples were cut open in search of harbingers. As quickly as a rose wilts, a person's life will pass. Girls tell fortunes from dandelions, pluck the petals of daisies, clap their hands with a rose petal inside and consider it a good omen when it bursts. The same superstition was documented in antiquity, which in turn inherited it from an even earlier time, so it can be assumed that some of these superstitions are thousands of years old. One of them is the custom of releasing wreaths to float down streams. Many other interpretations are connected with the shapes of branches and leaves, with the colors of trees and flowers, and with their names. We do not want to get stuck in the trap of ethnography, however, but to find or renew a bygone and needed relationship.

What Trees Dream About

Today, people often talk about their dogs. We feel clearly that sometimes a dog or, less frequently, a cat replaces a child or a partner and actually becomes (or so it seems to us) a substitute family member. We know from the rural literature of the nineteenth century that villagers talked in the same way about their cows, and that especially

* The word *bába* means "grandmother" in contemporary Czech, but originally meant "woman" or even "Woman" in the sense of female spirituality or a tree, or sometimes a stone in a shape of a menhir that embodies a female spirit.

goats were almost coequal family members. A girl would come in from the pasture and talk about what their goat was doing. When an aunt from the neighboring village came for a visit, she was immediately asked not only after her husband but also after their cow. For a city dweller, all the diffuse traditional ties to farm animals, fruit trees, soil, and the elements are concentrated into a single dog.

The second circle of family ties included favorite trees, and sometimes also springs and fields. People lived with them, observed them, and talked about them. And the trees paid them back in their own way.

*   *   *

When I was leaving for Amherst, Massachusetts, where Robert Frost once lived, I remembered his poem "The Telephone":

> When I was just as far as I could walk
> From here to-day,
> There was an hour
> All still
> When leaning with my head against a flower
> I heard you talk.
> Don't say I didn't, for I heard you say—
> You spoke from that flower on the window sill.

I told our little Eliška that maple trees have long roots that reach all the way to America, where they talk with the American maple trees. So if she wants to tell me something on the way to the nursery school, she should use the maple telephone, and I pointed to a full-grown Tatarian maple (*Acer tataricum*) in our park. It seemed strange to her; she had never heard of a maple telephone and so she did not use it. Nor did I learn anything about the goings-on at home from the maple trees in New England. Today we have mobile phones.

A Dream About the Spirit of a Tree

A dark tree is standing on a large plain above the horizon. Light is gleaming through the leaves. The tree is gently swinging, the lights change with the quivering. The tree is standing and shining. It is the spirit of the tree. It has no shape, no mind similar to mine. When the tree dies, the spirit moves somewhere else. In a forest this is easy, as it can strengthen the light of another tree, but in an open space the spirit slowly withers and dies out. This makes it unhappy, but it cannot help itself. It is neither good nor evil, but there is something majestic in it. Flittering light.

*   *   *

In the morning I realize that if I wanted to create a replica of the tree in my dream, it would look like a Christmas tree with shining round ornaments. Then I say to myself that if the light of a dying tree gives strength to the surrounding trees, then the forest's memory will last for thousands of years.

The Earth That Responds

When you descend toward Pastuchovice in western Bohemia from the south, you can turn off on a plateau above the village—first onto a field path at the edge of a forest and in a few meters into the interior of a deep woodland. The forest here is restless; many trees have been contorted repeatedly.

I worked in a landslide area for a few years and often looked around at the trees. When there's a slope movement causing a tree to lean over, it immediately corrects the imbalance by again aiming its trunk straight up. In landslide territory it's common for a tree to acquire a new equilibrium by expanding a branch that is inclined in the opposite direction into a new trunk, thereby creating a forked tree and evening out the force of gravity. By looking at the shape of the trunk, one can estimate the speed of the slope movement and whether it was a more or less fluid process or whether the sliding occurred in steps. On some slopes in the Central Bohemian Uplands we can observe the gradual bending of a trunk caused by a slow dragging movement down the slope of about forty centimeters over the past sixty years or so. This digression is just to make it clear that I know what a bent tree looks like.

About two hundred meters from the edge of the forest there is a strange formation. The trunks of trees in a circle of about fifty meters in diameter are all leaning toward a central point. The slender trunks of birches and pines are either crawling on the ground or bending toward the center like a tensed bow. The formation is less and less evident each year. For one thing, the locals seem to be trying to erase the traces of anything unusual by cutting off the strange branches. But the circle itself is transforming as well, as if a large vortex had swept through the landscape, and not for the first time. We slept in the circle and felt mildly restless, but had no visions, no mystical experiences; rather, we were amazed at some of the shapes of the trees. I said that if I was a Celt, I'd certainly erect an obelisk or altar here to some unknown restless god—maybe not even out of a sense of respect for the sacred, but because such things should not happen in a proper forest.

A year later I visited the Celtic oppidum in Třísov* and went straight to the northern acropolis. Several years earlier, statues of gods had stood here, erected in the 1990s by local Celt enthusiasts. But on the summit plateau there was no trace of them now. I'd be interested

---

* An oppidum is a Celtic proto-town. Large Celtic fortresses and settlements existed close to contemporary towns, including Závist south of Prague, the Celtic acropolis on the site of Bratislava Castle, and sacred Celtic sites near the hot springs below Gellért in Budapest or on Kahlenberg above Vienna.

to know what happened to them. Did they carry them back, or did someone destroy them because they did not understand them? I don't know, but the slim trunks of the birches were leaning in shapes resembling tensed bows toward the spot where the statues had stood, or perhaps the spot where people had stood in front of the statues. The shapes of the trunks matched those I had seen in Pastuchovice, but nowhere else.

Will stones call and trees bear witness even if people are silent? Or is the earth itself calling for something in its own quiet way when a stone talks very slowly with root hairs in the crevices of a rock? Something is going on here—some sort of quiet communication between the light of the rocks and the world of people, interpreted by trees. Shadows of gods and fingerprints of ancient peoples. As if an old man in a canvas hood was walking in front of me and then suddenly was there no more. Reflections, oh those reflections down there on the surface of the stream, green living dimness, if only it could speak. The conversations of leaves with the past, the oscillation of time, the same old man in the intertwined roots of alders, everything suddenly speaks in silence, the torsos of messages resembling dead birds, only the words are not discernible. A clear trill rises above the river and the stillness, the magic is interrupted. Just for a little while we enter a world that speaks of its own accord and gives rise in us to feelings, words, and songs. Where is the origin of all this, in what abyss of time and rock? In the knot of a luminous octopus floating freely inside the rock somewhere between Třísov and the golden heart of the earth?

A Revolution of Surface: 3
Successful as Asphalt

The success of the city as a social model is measurable in terms of the area it occupies—in Europe this is about 10 percent. If we were to measure the success of our civilization by percentages of surface area, we would arrive at a surprising conclusion: our civilization's most successful product is asphalt. Despite this, however, we would consider a characterization of singer Karel Gott or economist Václav Klaus* as "successful as asphalt" to be out of place. Similarly, we do not use similes such as "nice as a gas pump" or "ecological as malaria" either. Asphalt's success is invisible, as though asphalt itself did not exist. It is the city's gray background, against which more colorful scenes are acted out. It is like the screen in a cinema, which we stare at for the duration of the film and yet we do not perceive it, or even think about it. There are only very few books about asphalt and almost no poetry. If we cared to characterize it at all, we would probably mention its boring banality.

*   *   *

The person who is able to create something exciting out of asphalt could change the face of the world.

*   *   *

* Karel Gott is a popular Czech singer and Václav Klaus is a former president of the Czech Republic. Both are shrouded in a certain aura of banal fame, very different from real esteem or even greatness.

Scholarship has provided us with sufficient evidence of asphalt's ancient use as a means of insulation in buildings from the unfired bricks of Mohenjo-daro and the ziggurats of Sumer. From a modern point of view, however, these are mere oddities, which are in no way suggestive of asphalt's later success, which is more remarkable than splendid. Let's imagine a typical large European or American city at the end of the nineteenth century. We are familiar with numerous descriptions and photographs from this period. Surprisingly, architecture textbooks have a tendency to focus on buildings, but around them some 30–60 percent of a city's area constitutes roads (an example of the 60 percent figure is contemporary Los Angeles). From the point of view of the residents, however, the evolution of the sidewalk is more important than the development of ornamentation. Seen from a purely practical standpoint, in a city we make use of only a few buildings, but many streets. Thus, from a perspective on the city as a whole, its architecture is just as important as a city's surface, noise, or stench, but it is certainly not the whole city.

Testimonials about nineteenth-century cities combine memories of dust in the summer and mud during the rest of the year. With the exception of city centers, streets were not attractive for walks, but rather a necessary evil. Every animal, pedestrian, and vehicle was a potential whirlwind of dust. Harry Bulkeley Creswell described his memories of London in 1890 in the December 1958 issue of *Architectural Review* as essentially an overcrowded place—but the mud! The noise and stench!

Two Scotsmen: "Macadam" and "Mackintosh"

In his *Arcades Project*, Walter Benjamin noted that asphalt was first used for sidewalks. This was at some point around 1820. A decade later, asphalt was widely documented on the sidewalks of London and Paris, and somewhat thereafter in American cities as well. The first as-

Road near Slavonice

phalt was of natural origin. It was extracted in Trinidad, the Alps, and a number of other places. Although we use the common word *asphalt*, in reality it referred to a number of different bitumens of various compositions and with various properties. Equally varied was the technology of its processing. A good macadam road was made up of three layers of gravel: the largest stones were on the bottom and their size decreased gradually toward the surface. Very thin asphalt was repeatedly poured over the macadam so that it would flow as deep as possible and reinforce the bottom layer. The origin of the word *macadam* is similar to that of *mackintosh*. The former refers to John Loudon McAdam's invention of a special kind of gravel road around 1819, while the latter describes a waterproof fabric invented by Charles Macintosh around the same time (1823). It is a coincidence that Macintosh used tar from coal distillation similar to asphalt. It was a real asphalt period. Moreover, it rains a lot in Scotland, which contributes to the terrible roads there.

The asphalt sidewalk was a major innovation and was eagerly embraced. Not only did it make it possible for pedestrians to walk comfortably all over the city, it also insulated the city from perilous underground vapors, believed at the time to cause infectious disease. It also absorbed noise. Whereas today's roads reverberate with a deep and continuous hum, the streets of the nineteenth century resonated with horses' hooves and the clatter of steel felloes on the cobblestones. In 1961, Gordon Cullen suggested that cobblestone paving be reintroduced in cities for the sole reason of intimating to automobile drivers that they were not welcome there.

The path to the asphalt road took two more decades. Asphalt softened in the summer heat and was deformed by the narrow felloes of carriages and hackneys. By 1850, asphalt was already a common sight in the streets of Berlin and other European cities. Émile Zola, Gustave Flaubert, and Guy de Maupassant welcomed it with joy as a unique material for promenades. Their heroes and heroines could finally discuss matters of the heart right in the streets without concern over which puddle they might step into. Asphalt created the space for a new kind of social interaction: the urban and later also the suburban street. Somewhat later, asphalt also created the street as a children's playground. This is no longer true; no one plays ball in the street anymore, no one makes chalk drawings in the street, and no one plays hopscotch. Asphalt giveth and asphalt taketh away.*

The Bitumen Religion

In the 1920s, the car posters of one Italian automobile club featured not only cars but also asphalt. Both were symbols of progress—after all, a modern means of transportation had to glide along a smooth, dust-free surface. Moreover, asphalt and gasoline went well together. Long gone were the days when asphalt was mined or extracted from asphalt lakes; now it was a by-product of oil refining. The symbiosis was almost perfect—at least from the point of view of the man behind the wheel, but less so from that of the pedestrian.

Spaces paved with asphalt were increasingly the domain of automobiles, which pushed the pedestrians out. Cars in many cities were originally parked in the rear, in renovated horse stables, but as the automobile became a symbol of prestige and wealth—something to be displayed for the neighbors to see—parking moved to the areas in front of houses. This brought about something that Mirko Zardini calls "an excess of success." It was as though asphalt became part of a new bitumen religion of modernity. Mud was medieval, cobblestone paving was aristocratic, but asphalt was the right surface for democracy and, later, also for class struggle. Shooting into crowds of students and workers is best done on asphalted spaces. One Czech adage deprecates the paver as obscene, but there is no comparable saying relating

---

* The inspiration for this essay is Mirko Zardini's essay "Surface of the City," in *Sense of the City: An Alternative Approach to Urbanism* (Montreal: Canadian Centre for Urbanism, 2005). It is very important, however, to protect old asphalt roads and sidewalks, as in Košice (Slovakia) where part of an early twentieth-century sidewalk constructed by a British company is protected as cultural heritage.

to the asphalter, for he is a man of progress. Gone are the days when Jože Plečnik,* who loved warm materials such as ceramics, dared to use asphalt for the floor of a church.

The Semiotic Value of Asphalt

In the 1960s, asphalt began to be perceived as an enemy. It constrained pedestrians, and absorbed solar energy on hot days only to radiate it at night, thus turning the city into an urban heat island. Where there was asphalt, no grass would grow. The smooth surface enabled the wind to pick up speed and whirl up a vortex of dust and trash. Asphalt-covered areas drained water much faster, thus increasing the risk of flooding. Asphalt became a substitute for more elegant materials such as stone and thus became associated with poor neighborhoods. At the same time, its semiotic value was increasing, as it could be used as a palimpsest for children's chalk drawings as well as the medium on which the crosswalks and other traffic markers could be painted. Traffic markers probably first appeared on asphalt in 1919 in Boston during a strike by traffic policemen, who thought chaos would ensue if they stopped directing the traffic flow. The literary analysis of texts written on asphalt demonstrates their striking emotional crudeness and the prevalence of commands and prohibitions over positive statements such as "Oh, the times of the Great Pyramid!"

Recent decades have seen the rise of various movements of asphalt destroyers who pride themselves on the amount of inhospitable area they have converted back into lawns. It sounds immensely appeal-

---

* Jože Plečnik (1872–1957) was a Slovenian architect and a friend of the first Czechoslovak president, Tomáš Garrigue Masaryk, who employed him to change the spirit of Prague Castle from an aristocratic center to the seat of a democratic state. Plečnik used asphalt for the church floor and sewage system tubes as pillars in sacral buildings. He refused to take a salary for this project in order to be totally independent. Plečnik and the president's daughter shared affections for one another, but ultimately decided to forgo a romantic relationship in favor of their shared passion for Prague Castle: architecture as an act of love and sacrifice.

ing—to destroy that ugly gray asphalt, the enemy of life. But let's take it a step further. I would like to mention two things that in my opinion are important:

> ✒ Monument preservation is concerned almost exclusively with buildings, but in certain places it would be interesting to preserve historical asphalt (and other) surfaces because they contain part of the history of modern civilization, although not a part with which we are enamored—the victory of grayness and automobile culture.
>
> ✒ We are very unconcerned with the aesthetics of asphalt, because we consider it a banal and rather negative material. If, however, we consider the fact that—in terms of surface area—asphalt constitutes the largest part of modern civilization, that we cannot escape it, and that to do so is not desirable because asphalt is practical, is elastic, and dampens noise, it becomes clear that the person who develops a "new asphalt" will change the visual appeal of cities and of all of civilization. Asphalt has another great characteristic—it can be easily and efficiently recycled. This will be of great interest when the prices of oil and oil products increase.

Attempts to change the look of asphalt have so far taken two approaches. The first is to color the asphalt surface and the second is to use structured materials, for example a mixture of straw and asphalt, which can be used as insulating plaster. Another possibility is apparent around the edges of poorly maintained asphalt surfaces. On a softer substrate the asphalt layer develops cracks, like drying mud, where grass grows, so even an asphalt surface has something natural about it and can absorb precipitation.

*   *   *

I would almost say that asphalt still has its best years ahead of it.

Journey to Uničov or About the Gap Between the Birds

You Can't Force the Universe

After some hesitation over the town of Litovel, I found the town of Uničov* on a map of the Czech Republic. I had repeatedly promised to travel there and meet with people in the local library. The smaller and more remote a town is, the happier people are when someone comes. It's not worth the effort to give lectures in oversaturated Prague, but in a town where, as one local noted quite unjustly, there are just two big social events a year—the Jára Cimrman Theater and the Travesti Show**—people make strudel for you or bring you a jar of homemade honey. A lecture in a small town, if possible in the backcountry and especially in the foothills of the Low Jeseník Mountains, is a reason for people to come from as far away as Rýmařov in northern Moravia, some five hours by train from Prague—partly because of what you have to say, but also because they need to meet up with friends and revive cultural and social networks beyond the scope

---

* Uničov is a small town in northern Moravia, unknown and possibly incomprehensible to the intellectuals of Prague but still a "middle of somewhere." Litovel is several miles from Uničov.

** The Jára Cimrman Theater is a Prague theater company that creates and produces plays about the exploits of Jára Cimrman, a fictional Czech genius who lived in the late nineteenth and early twentieth centuries. The Travesti Show is a transvestite semi-striptease.

of the Travesti Show. Moreover, Magris, the local wise woman, had said she was sure I would come, because she had requested this of the universe. But as she put it: "It works, but you can't force it." People in Prague, Brno, or Ostrava have their acquaintances, their political or shady contacts, but one feels better among people who would have relied on St. Florian in the previous century and who now rely on the universe, which is—as tends to be acknowledged somewhat unwillingly—larger than the European Union.

In the morning I wake up both sad and happy, like a man who has lost a piece of diamond jewelry, or whose jewel went off on its own ill-fated way (like the Saudi blue diamond), who knows, but now there's no need to worry about it anymore, and after all it was too precious to be of any use anyway. I slide a thick European Institute for Security Studies report into my backpack entitled "The New Global Puzzle: What World for the EU in 2025?" When I later ask the audience in Uničov what they would be interested in, the first question is what Europe will look like in twenty years. One may underestimate the current political scene, but not the universe and its wise women.

Not Everything Is Art, and Thank God for That

I get off the train in Šternberk, because I've never been there. The town is reviving, but one can still feel that the war ended not long ago—repaired cobblestone paving, but battered houses and architecturally discordant garages built by post-1945 settlers. A mixture of the new, clean Europe and the Sudetenland.* A smiling old lady says with resignation: "There's a big difference between the Sudetenland in Bo-

---

* The Sudetenland consists of the mostly hilly border regions of Czech territory where German-speaking people lived until 1945, when they were expelled. It is still a rather cold belt of land which accepts newcomers with reluctance and suspicion.

hemia and in Moravia! In Bohemia there's at least something going on, some remedy has at least begun, but here the region is just falling apart right before your eyes. The last regime—God forbid that it should return—at least maintained the bus connections, a network of miserable supermarkets and attending dentists." I take the underpass leading beneath the square and head toward the church. On the way, I pass the municipal gallery and notice a poster advertising a Marián Palla exhibition that I'd wanted to see, but I hadn't made it all the way out to Opava where the opening had taken place. I enter the gallery together with two youths whom an enlightened local teacher has assigned to visit this exhibition. The admission is five Czech crowns*— yes, the region is this backward. The gallerist is visibly surprised by the number of visitors; he is not used to such crowds here and welcomes us enthusiastically.

Marián Palla (b. 1953 in Košice) is the kind of person who, if he had to burn a CD, would do so in a microwave. He studied at the conservatory in Brno and then played the string bass at the Brno Opera for a long time. I know what he's doing now, but I won't write it here out of consideration. In Šternberk he exhibited the empty beer bottles he had consumed during the exhibition's installation. Beneath one of his drawings he wrote: "I walked through the countryside, but since I had cigarettes, it was bearable." I stop in front of a painting entitled *A Great Love and a Small Bird*. The boys hesitate quite visibly at a painting divided in two halves marked *Painted During the Day* and *Painted During the Night*. Gathering their courage, they address me: "Sir, could you tell us something about it?" I show them the line: "It took Mr. Palla 24 uninterrupted hours to paint this line. During that entire time he did not remove the brush from the painting. He wore a kind of skirt that was slit at the bottom so he could use the chamber pot, which was emptied by visitors."

---

* Five crowns is equivalent to about thirty cents.

The boys shake their heads in disbelief. I continue: "And in the morning he also drank tea with a stone. He sat and from time to time he spilled tea on it. Or he mixed the tea with dirt and splashed it over the picture in a happy moment. Or he sat and kneaded earth, or he traveled to the Low Tatras to touch a stone. He also went to the fields and the forests to record the dimensions of sticks and stones, in order to learn something about himself and about philosophy. Then he got lost in his own self because he did a kind of art that hid him from himself. Nonetheless, his friends got the impression from the notes he didn't write that he was a great artist." I continue: "You know, here we are in Šternberk, and what you are looking at seems like a joke, but this exhibition (unlike almost all other exhibitions in the Czech Republic) could be displayed in the best Parisian galleries. You don't know what you've got here and I don't blame you."

I feel that I should explain this, and continue on: "Once he sent a watering can full of water from Brno to Opava, and at the opening the curator poured it out on the floor. It was clear that it was a *different* kind of water and that one could do very *simple* things with it. Another time he painted a decent abstract painting and wrote on it in large red letters 'Spoiled Painting.' He also painted with dirt and then wrote on it 'probably only dirt' because he could not be sure he hadn't added something to it. On another similar painting he wrote 'only breath and earth.' He tried to wait alone, but then he waited with a stone. He wanted to rescue an abandoned *animal* and write a novel. He also longed for a tractor he could repair all the time to keep him from just shitting his life away."

I take a deep breath: "And he was also a member of the group Měkkohlaví. They wrote a manifesto according to which the main condition of membership was to hate the members of other groups. They were not allowed—except for the chairman—to paint snouts. They had to recognize their own work, but they were also allowed to praise the works of the other members of the group. They had to paint as much as they could, so that nobody could say they were lazy, and they had to exhibit it as soon as possible in order to be popular. Besides that, he wrote a few books, including a Western about treacherous Indians who conspired with Radiata from some flying saucer."

The boys, initially bored by the assignment, are now hanging on my every word and waiting for more outrageous stories. I start to wrap up, saying that if we had more time, we could talk about something I myself don't know, namely about what Tao is. I don't know it, but I can *recognize where there's a bit of it and where there's not enough*. Wang-Pi, the first great commentator on the *Tao Te Ching*, said that if people exist just for themselves, they will clash with others, but if they exist for others, the others will come to them of their own accord. "It's enough that you are here. Maybe some day you'll buy an old tractor and succumb to Zen Buddhism."

Placing a Ring of Light on the Underground River of Divination

Uničov is a project that didn't work out right. While most medieval towns were founded at some point after 1250, Uničov gained its town privileges in 1223, that is, a couple of decades before Prague. The Přemyslids* believed the town would give them access to the ore deposits in the Jeseníky Mountains, because extensive mining of iron ore deposits (and possibly of silver and gold deposits as well) was already under way here well before AD 1000. Uničov could have become a second capital in the northern half of Moravia after Olomouc, but its

---

* The Přemyslids were a Bohemian royal dynasty that reigned in Bohemia, Moravia, and other territories from the ninth century until 1306. It was the first ruling dynasty of the Kingdom of Bohemia (1198–1918).

significance has gradually been declining since the Thirty Years' War. From the beginning it was a German town, as was often the case with settlements in the foothills associated with mining and trade. In 1900 only 2 percent of its residents claimed to be of Czech origin. Konrad Henlein* received a warm welcome here at the beginning of World War II. The resulting situation, however, resembled that in the German Democratic Republic after the Wall came down: "arrogant colleagues from the West" were assigned to important posts. In the case of Uničov, it was people from the Reich, and so life in the town continued down the customary path: big dreams became small hopes, and the war economy affected everyone. The youth had to work for local farmers to secure food supplies for the front, and in the evenings they received political education. By 1944 it had become clear that Uničov had allowed itself to become involved in a great misunderstanding.

I would like to have seen the end of the war in Uničov and the sobering up of the small, ordinary Germans who so resembled the small, ordinary Moravians. It must have been dismal. The people caught and denounced their own German deserters who were executed almost daily at Šibeník. On May 5, General Schörner** still wanted to fortify the town and wage a battle with the Russians. Mayor Franz Siegel refused. He resigned, went home, shot his wife, and hanged himself. Then it was like a bad dream. It was as though a howling wind of hopelessness was blowing through the town, as though the spirit of the ending war had beguiled the people and swelled with much greater power than had been attributed to it historically. The German inhabitants fled the town in a panic. And here's something I'm at a loss to explain: eighty-one local residents committed suicide! Is it even possible to imagine such horror in a

* Konrad Henlein (1898–1945) was a prominent Sudeten German politician in interwar Czechoslovakia. Following the German invasion, he joined the Nazi Party and served as governor of the Sudetenland (1939–1945).
** Ferdinand Schörner (1892–1973) was a field marshal in the German army known for his brutality. A committed Nazi, he was one of Hitler's favorite commanders.

small agricultural town? Or were some of those suicides actually murders for property and retribution?

I didn't sense any of this in the town, however. I had the impression that Uničov was a rather peaceful and happy place at the end of the Haná plains and the beginning of the Jeseníky foothills, a town of ordinary, diligent people—no magic knot of unknown forces. If the aliens chose to land in Uničov, I would be surprised, whereas in other places, like Kladno near Prague or Loket in western Bohemia not far from Karlovy Vary—each for entirely different reasons—I would consider it absolutely normal.

*   *   *

After the lecture I'm sitting with Magris the wise woman and several locals in a pub. She holds back for a while, but then energetically breaks into conversation about numbers and stars. She analyzes the date of my birth and in so doing connects with some basis of what I am, which means that for a moment we touch and exchange parts of ourselves. The gap between the flying birds is not filled by air, but by the balancing of one's own weight and mutual proximity, which has many forms. I answer her by quoting Gustav Meyrink's parable about a tree that secretly grows inside a person, only to become suddenly visible with its branches, heavy with fruit, reaching far beyond the fence of the self. Slightly taken by her prophetic air, I do not force the universe. I tell her that she, unlike most other people, is on a vivacious path, that she will continue and live on the edge like all good witches, but that she will be saved by her own inner honesty (which she has) and by the books she is presently working with.

The Pythian nature has the instinctive essence of ground waters that, after years of calm, tend to want to set off on unexpected paths, some of which lead to madness. She knows it. The glow of letters, the wafting of refined intellect, the touch of books, something we call culture places a ring of light on the underground rivers of imagination and divination. It is clear to her, just a matter of taking the books in your hands with a gesture that returns the potential demons to their places. She looks at me: "You have recapitulated a bit of my horoscope in other words."

In the Manor Jail

In a side street there's an old manor jail, for which we have the keys. Midnight is approaching. I pull out a flashlight and we slowly walk through the small building containing several cells. It is neither romantic nor eerie. It's an ordinary jail from which people went home or to the gallows. Various inscriptions, names, the figure of a small deer, several signs, and years have been scrawled into the doors. Opposite the cells there is the narrow space of the solitary: a black hole without windows that emanates fear and powerlessness. German books and official decrees from the nineteenth century lie scattered in the attic. Little calligraphic signs are decorated in dark oak-apple ink.

No plot is ascending toward a climax; the essay is not culminating in a conclusion. To the contrary, the world is calming down and finally has nothing to say. We walk through Uničov by night, wave good-bye in this average town. Neither shadows, nor lights. I go to bed thinking about Jorge Luis Borges, who may have once heard a bird singing by night on the outskirts of Barracas, and felt compassion just exactly in the size of that bird.

Walking through a landscape we experience a calm unlike the city, an indefinite sanctity in its configuration, a depth of time in its geological layers, and a sense that this earth was touched by generations of our ancestors and that some part of them has been absorbed into the earth and that some part of the earth has been absorbed into us. We can renew our roots only at home, certainly not in any of the globalized regions. And so we sometimes feel grief over the landscape that we are losing under a network of highways, suburban developments, and industrial warehouses full of things that in the end we do not need. We are interested in order only when one order ends and we fear the next. Once freedom was an obsession for us, and so we roamed without any particular destination in mind; today, freedom is a source of stress and we need to learn who we are and where we belong, and this is why we wander. The tourist wants to see things, the vagabond experiences freedom, but the wanderer seeks to be transformed. Do you think the dogs, trees and landscape will denounce us on Judgment Day?

I'm calling you, but you're laughing. A landscape for a dwarf and a tree as a tutor? You're looking for a universal language and you find it at a point where a path scattered with pink granite meets a path covered with grayish phyllite—what's that supposed to mean? I explain patiently: the main dwarves—for us the most important ones—

have worn red caps since antiquity. Originally they lived in the center of the house—and consequently also in the center of the family—beneath the hearth. They still wear the red reflection of the flames on their heads. A house without a spirit protector did not have anyone to stand up for it in those parts of the Sixth Heaven where counsels are born. The spirit was actually a family ancestor firmly bound to the fire of one specific hearth; if this fire was allowed to burn out, the spirit could have been punished with banishment or even death. Can't you see that a dwarf in a red cap is holding the roots of your order in his strong hands, and at a time when the world is changing?

And it's a world full of words that no longer say anything. Whom do you want to ask and who is supposed to teach you a certain devotion, natural rhythm, and free-flowing time? The news on television, or a colorful maple tree with palmate leaves in your garden? And if we are to play the game of where we belong, what do we answer? We belong to the language of our mothers, and the two may coalesce for us at a certain age. Then we belong to the books that we've read and whose knowledge we've shared with others. We belong to the deep caves or even crypts where we realized who we might become, and from these depths we climb up to high places and look out over the landscape of our home. When I'm home, I know where I am. Landscape is a special type of garden straddling nature and man; it is tamed nature. It is like our tomcat—no longer a wild beast, but something between a predator and a plush toy. Landscape garden, organized chaos, the permanent fertile rebellion of old gods against new orders; the garden anarchist with Japanese eyes and fair Nordic hair is singing its own song of granite and moss, and we look on.

We are no longer concerned with what is beautiful and what is merely prestigious. In a landscape garden we come to ourselves, time slows down, and we perceive that space is not given to us in and of itself; rather, it must be created and renewed. And for that, we have a shovel, shears, and speech. A community emerges of people, trees,

Carp pond in Dačice

and extremely unreliable birds who, despite all we have done to them, constantly—albeit somewhat derisively—strive to make contact with us. And sometimes in the evening, in the autumn fog when the faded sun is dissolving the haze behind the sycamore, we sense that we are not alone here, and the garden with no space for a dwarf, the pond where there can be no fairy, and the stone which is so reticent that it is no longer calm, that it is almost nothing at all—this is when we know that such a place is becoming an empty scene and that it matters little whether we are in a garden or an airport terminal. And so we check the outer garden—whether it has enough moisture and nitrates, and while doing so we notice that the inner garden is missing a bit of calm, a pinch of home, and one dwarf. We remedy everything with an affable chat, lie down in the grass, and gaze up into the sky through the leaves. And then, maybe only for a while, we are given a sense of the order that never disappeared, the wandering that has just reached its destination, the calm that is not fatigue—and we know that we exist and that it is not bad at all.

Tranquility at the Fundaments of the World   6

All around us, speed overcomes slow movement, noise drowns out silence, and politics triumphs over culture. But looking back into the past, this is not the case. Over a longer time span, only the sediment of a smile, tranquility, and a certain weight remain of a proud and brutal history. How this is possible, we don't know. When reminiscing about the past, we remember musicians and poets, but not bankers and police chiefs. We hardly remember two or three names of ministers who were in office twenty or thirty years ago, but we know dozens of books, films, and melodies from the same period. Maybe the world of the past is created by radiography. We have the feeling that soothingly melancholic tranquility will ultimately overpower almost everything—the swinging, the turmoil, and maybe even the horror, and that it lies somewhere at the fundaments of the world and will remain there in the end.

What mystery has befallen us?
—John of Damascus

The Mental Morphology of the Unhuman

Poet František Dryje, the author of *Požíraný druh* (Eaten Species), said that Vratislav Effenberger* presumed that the consciousness of man is not determined as much by the various traumas and deprivations of childhood as by the landscape in which the child lived and the objects he touched. Years ago, surrealists even used questionnaires in an attempt to prove that the way the landscape is shaped, how many nooks and recesses a house has, and how crooked the tree in front of the window is all have the same influence on the psyche as one's upbringing. The surrealists called this imprint of the external form, this set of measurable magnitudes, dimensions, tones, and colors in the spiritual microcosm of the child his *mental morphology*. At least this is how I understood it when I remembered how many poets and painters carry with them the courtyards, the staircases, the insides of

---

* František Dryje and Vratislav Effenberger are Czech surrealists who always lived in order to live, and not in order to create. Czech surrealism is a rather uncertain but rich approach to how to live.

wardrobes, the brooks and trees of their childhood as the decisive element of their inner state of mind (*collocatio*).

We are and are not humans. The soul is a collection, just like the body. The backbone was invented by the graptolites of the Silurian, breathing originated in the bacterial stages of the earth's development somewhere in the deep Archean, bones appeared in the reptiles of the Permian, warm-blooded organisms and blood as such emerged in the Mesozoic. We are like a portrait by Giuseppe Arcimboldo, assembled from numerous "natural artifacts," each of them a piece of history, a story, and spirituality. We expend great amounts of time and energy to hold together this menagerie, botanical garden, and also the universe (*and also the universe!!!*): the lizards, the sycamore, and the stars, all arranged in some functional and logical order. We will not concern ourselves now with the fact that the way in which things are arranged in an edifice inside us must be geometrical, or—more precisely—morphological, and that consequently some relationship between the inner and outer morphology is to be expected; rather, we will consider the way in which the menagerie is addressed.

As humans we are addressed by our superiors, televisions, spouses, and human folly. But it seems as if every item in our collection is addressed (especially when the paper of our lives is still absorbent) by a corresponding thing in the outer world: the material of the stairs we climbed, the coarseness of the bark of our favorite tree (it had slipped my mind, but as I am writing, I realize it was not forgotten), the feathers of birds. There are two plots unfolding at the same time here. Humans must function just like a city must function—as a whole. But in every neighborhood and every house the inhabitants live their lives that flow into the gush of consciousness of the city and sometimes shift it in a different direction. They change its organization and give it a different axis, as when you accept a totem animal, start taking family life seriously, or convert to Catholicism.

🦎 *Cubist Stair, House of the Black Madonna, Prague*

The Man with the Soul of a Moose and
the Moose with the Soul of a Moose

In Krtola Cave near Mužský* we dug a two-meter trench in an effort to reach the bedrock and to determine, based on the sediments, the circumstances under which the cave had been formed. Encircled by flying horseshoe bats and crammed into badger dens—that is, in a place addressing our menagerie—we talked about how more and more people were dreaming about animals. I think this is due to the revival of Native American culture feeding the human subconscious with images from times when animals were our comrades and teachers. Then one of the diggers began reminiscing about his last trip to the Kounov Stone Alignments.

The Kounov Alignments** almost always disappoint. Only on the immense overturned stone called Pegas does the sacred breathe. The fourteen rows cutting across the Džbán plain have, I think, the ritual function of protecting the place that lies beyond them. Focusing only on the rows is like focusing only on the ramparts of a town, reflecting on them, and not entering the town itself. Behind them lies a small, originally Romanesque church and an ancient fortified settlement, which has been inhabited intermittently for at least two millennia (which is twice the time historical Prague has existed). The edges of the plain are extraordinarily prone to block slides. The sandstone and marl plate is sinking into the subjacent clays and is sliding into the valley in blocks and swaths twenty to thirty meters across. The earth is again beginning to tear near the settlement behind the Kou-

---

* Krtola Cave is a prehistoric sandstone cave in Bohemian Paradise, a protected natural area northeast of Prague known for its sandstone cliffs.
** The Kounov Stone Alignments are an enigmatic structure composed of several thousand small stones of unknown origin and age possibly related to a nearby Early Iron Age fortification or cultic site. Contemporary stories about flying lights, invisible hands gently touching one's hands in the night, or even a black earth dragon are common there.

nov Alignments, and the western slope bears the scar of a slide. The block that is gradually detaching from the plain has created a small gorge of sorts—a rill about twenty meters long and five meters deep at its deepest point, but only about one meter wide. A small arch and cave were formed here from the piled stones. I won't go into describing the local pseudokarst. It suffices to say that at this ancient, possibly sacred, and most probably also well-guarded place, the earth opened up, exposing the entrance to its roots, and images rise up from the underworld.

The digger told us this story:

I connected my dream with a descent into the gorge, as though I had imbibed it there, in *that place*. I slept in a sort of stone shelter among small, brown, slender people. I don't quite belong there, but they are friendly, skillful, and agile; they smile, and live together. We are walking along a slope, wading in fallen leaves. There is a small rock formation opposite us and we hear footsteps. We're curious what kind animal it is; we're expecting a doe. Then something large and brown appears—a young moose with short palmate antlers. I'm glad to see a moose, I've always wanted to see one, but they disappeared from our region at some point in the fifteenth century and today they're returning only very slowly, for example in the Třeboň area. The moose makes a majestic impression; it's beautiful. It rushes by, and we greet it with a smile and admiration. It almost disappears from view, but then returns. A moment of fear—does it want to attack us? It stops in front of us. It has the large, ironic, and knowing eyes of a magician. They might penetrate us, but we're not worth the effort. Then it tosses its head and from behind we can see that it has one more face, but this one is covered with a wooden mask, attached with leather straps. The mask is round like that of the moon and behind it we sense a being from the Cernunnos* lineage, or from the miracle of St. Hubert. Why didn't anyone tell us that it was the god of deer who had appeared to Hubert? I'm quite shaken and part of my geometry needs to be re-created.

Recently at the end of a philosophical seminar, one esteemed philosopher, whose name I cannot recall (Václav Bělohradský?) uttered the axiomatic sentence that "man is a transcendental being." This is usually understood to mean that humanity transcends toward God, but looking at my own collection and seeing the world around me, I would say that humans also transcend toward the deer, the raven, the trees and stones. But the moose must be a transcendental being, too, and moss must have something of the stone's spirituality. But does the moose transcend toward us? An answer suggests itself: "Why would it?"

I haven't run across the local witch in the woods near Sedlice in eastern Slovakia, who is remembered to this day as Medová baba (Old Honey Woman), but I have an inkling about what the essence of her wisdom was. It wasn't in the technical description of her magic potions, but in her ability to communicate with what lurks behind the owl or lady's mantle. The ability to cause one specific thing from the outer landscape to resonate with the sick part of the collection. That's when the world began to speak all languages. I was glad that I had my own and that it was of a geometrical lineage.

---

* Cernunnos is the "horned god" of Celtic polytheism.

Don't Let Yourself Be Danced Down, Don't Journey to the Roots, Don't Cross Borders, Don't Dream!

We're carrying out inventory research in the Blanský Forest Protected Landscape Area.* In the upper section of the stream flowing toward Chvalšiny there's a marshland of connected rivulets. The stream flows out of a closed floodplain, leaves a degree of granulate debris, and creates small terraced bogs composed of fine brown sandy earth, similar to the dust loams that accumulated at the end of the last ice age. The central meadow of the alluvial plain is bordered by a spruce forest of inferior quality. Beyond it lie the overflowing rapids of a clearly ringing river. We delight in the humble, yet beautiful snowbells blooming in violet. The sharp stems of a rare white veratrum shoot up by the stream.

Veratrum album. The green maiden. Its appearance is majestic and awe inspiring. One senses its sacredness, as if the veratrum were not alone in this world. There is someone who knows its every leaf. There is a power behind it, knowing and kind, but which can also become unkind. The green maiden is moody, but Medová baba knows how to talk to her and how to impress her will upon her. The green maiden obeys, but will forget if she meets something closer to her nature. Her responsibility doesn't reach as far as humans; she doesn't care. The green maiden has within her something of a bygone lover. She danced away with part of a soul. This botany is about growing together: arms change into branches, and legs become attached to the stones. The white veratrum doesn't reach up to a man; it is the man who bows down. Don't let yourself be danced down, don't journey to the roots, don't cross borders, don't dream! A green fog descends. The man returns and stutters when expected to speak. This is not a good and safe path. Better to start with rye; it's tame and yet it remembers.

---

* Blanský Forest is a protected landscape area in southern Bohemia famous for its beech forests.

The Sacred Places of Deer

We're hiking along the Bralná Fatra section of Greater Fatra.*
The meadows on the ridges are ancient; humans had already created
pastures here by the end of the Bronze Age three thousand years ago.
The forest, destroyed in the nineteenth century by pasturing and
lumber harvesting, is nothing special; it's really just trees more than
a forest—bushes and low dolomite rocks, an unpleasant shrub layer.
We go around rock debris. A bear passed by here not long ago—the
droppings are fresh and the bark has recently been scratched off a tree.
I find a piece of a deer skull. It looks like a modified mask with two
openings for eyes. I put it in front of my face and gaze at the surrounding landscape through the eyes of a deer. This will prepare me for the
place beyond the next peak.

We come to a glade between two rocks about fifty meters apart.
It offers a view of the other side of the valley in the distance. Our feet
stop of their own accord. In the middle of the clearing, there's an irregular ellipse some six meters in diameter. The grass here has been
grazed so frequently that it has the appearance of a manicured lawn,
but the edge of the circle is well defined. Even from a distance, this
edge can be located down to a few centimeters. The ground has been
trodden by the hooves of deer; the air is filled with their scent. They
lie here and observe the valley. Every now and then they take a bite of
grass. Humans hardly ever come here. I feel as though I am invading
the intimacy of this space—and again that strong feeling of sacredness, as if I were in the cathedral of the deer. What do deer believe
in? In the Mother of all deer, who gives them grass, warmth and the
ability to survive the winter? I've seen dogs who believed in their masters—bewildered, angry, and joyful animals—cats stressed by travel,
and guinea pigs communicating intently with the hand feeding them

* Greater Fatra or Velká Fatra is a limestone mountain range in central Slovakia formerly used for grazing sheep.

grass, animals with all kinds of feelings. Why should the feeling of sacredness be lacking among them, and why should there be a need to replenish it? I'll never know what deer believe in, but I respect it and hold it in high regard.

Ilya Muromets and Svyatogor

In this mental morphology we descend far deeper than childhood experience and psychoanalysis, to somewhere in the memory of our species. Dušan Třeštík brought me an old Russian book with an amazing analysis of what we consider to belong to us and what we consider to belong to others. It's all based on the rather unclear legend of the unhuman, of Svyatogor.

In the borderlands of the Russian country, where the inhabited region touches the mountains and the recesses settled by various tribes, people recount the legend of a powerful mountain graybeard called Svyatogor, who must be killed because he is not of human lineage, and everything unhuman threatens the integrity of our civilization. Svyatogor himself does neither good nor wrong. His bones grow through the rocks and when he moves, creasing occurs. Just try spending a week in the mountains lying on the ground, listening for whether an old man who is not of our kind isn't moving about beneath the surface. It's an abysmal experience, a moment that can change the geometry of one's soul. But we have a system of guards who filter our experiences, so nothing will happen; we just went crazy for a split second, but now everything is fine again.

Ilya Muromets visits him. The old man asks himself what kind of mosquito is crawling on his back. Svyatogor is slow, almost immobile; there is no struggle, just the slow clubbing to death of the old man, who has no idea what it is all about. Is this Russian or human mentality? The Czechs and the Bavarians moved their giants out of

Šumava, albeit with occasional blunders, as with the expulsion of the Germans from Czechoslovakia. In the European tradition the unhuman is displaced to the mountains, the caves, or sacred regions, but it's never beaten to death. Unhuman things threaten us, but if we get rid of them, we cease to be human—Toyen* rid of the seaside calm. What is human in us is the way we organize the unhuman.

Venusians in Suchomasty

The story I'd like to tell is concerned with how legends emerge in our times. I was there and experienced the region still filled with excitement, but today no one remembers it anymore. It seems we take things that don't belong in our world, lock them away in an iron chest, and throw the key down the drain, and yet they are still here and influence us. It's a story of the unhuman, and I cannot explain it—how could pears tell you something about apples? It's the most complicated and extraordinary story I've ever heard and I doubt I'll ever hear anything like it.

There was a time when I used to go dig in the Koněprusy Caves** every two or three weeks. It was and still is my habit to stop by and visit Ms. J. for cake. She was a teacher at the time and knew personally the children who encountered the Venusians (this is the name the inhabitants of Suchomasty gave them), as well as their parents. All wonder-struck, she told me the story: three boys left school a little earlier than usual. They went to the plain above Suchomasty to a place where there is a swamp surrounded by reeds. It lies a bit below the headwaters of the Suchomasty stream, which drains part

---

* Toyen is the pseudonym of Marie Čermínová (1902–1980), a Czech surrealist painter.
** The Koněprusy Caves are a set of caves open for public tours and located in the Czech Karst some forty kilometers southwest of Prague. The area is famous for a high concentration of prehistoric settlements and folk legends describing miraculous white and golden horses.

Homemade drain, Slavonice

of the area in the foreland of Čertovy schody and which has a stable higher temperature of about ten degrees Celsius year-round. The boys wanted to catch some newts there. They climbed up to the road leading from Koněprusy, which branches out in several directions at two crossroads. The swamp lies right below the crossroads in the direction of Vinařice. No sooner were they on the road than they looked in the direction of Bykoš and saw something extremely humorous.

Approaching them on the road at high speed were three grotesque beings. The funny thing was in particular that they had one foot on the road and were rapidly pumping with the other, as when you ride a kick scooter. The beings were arranged in a triangular formation. If I remember correctly, the one in front was green and the two in back were brown. They were wearing strange clothes that continued upward into hoods like those worn by the Ku Klux Klan. Their eyes were large and glassy. It was amusing until the beings came right up to them, and the boys noticed that the formation was moving through the air—that is, they were gliding about half a meter off the ground. The beings then picked up speed and vanished in the distance. Terror-stricken, the boys left their bottles and fled home. One of them fell asleep from exhaustion and when he awoke, he told this rather improbable story so convincingly that his parents called the state police—Veřejná bezpečnost, which under the Communist regime was something one tried to avoid if possible. And if you called them over a story like this, your conviction must have been very strong.

The officers then checked the boys' accounts. How far away were they standing, can you show me how much five meters is, and so on. It lasted for another whole day and no one was allowed to talk about it. The accounts were said to be consistent. But that's not all, even though it will sound improbable. That same day a prisoner had escaped from the uranium mines in Příbram. This happened from time to time, and it was always the talk of the town. Officers were stationed at every major crossroads. The crossroads above and below the site of the encounter with the Venusians had been under surveillance, and no one saw a thing. It was absurd to think that the Venusians just materialized for a two-kilometer ride and then vanished again. On the one hand there was the boys' experience, and on the other there was this strange coincidence that it occurred at a rare moment (which only happens about once a decade) when it could be reliably ruled out.

I concluded that it is the nature of part of this world to confront us with riddles that can't be solved, to show something quite clearly and then to hide it again. Other than that, there's nothing sensible one can say about it. The story avoids the usual stereotypes of superstition—no dwarves, treasure, or white maidens; instead, strange beings, terrifying yet laughable, riding an invisible kick scooter half a meter off the ground, and nothing more.

Last year I went to the Koněprusy Caves with my students and Ms. J. When we were in the Prošek Dome I reminded her of the story. She was startled and said, "Ah yes, I never remember that."

Dreaming About Vigilance:
A Nut from Nine
Undersea Hazel Trees

For several years the admirable Josef Ryzec organized exhibitions of paintings and sculptures with Celtic themes at Vyšehrad for the Celtic feast of Lughnasadh. This was accompanied by draft beer and music by the band Kukulín or the like. These events had a peculiar atmosphere, funny yet serious; Josef was obviously up to something, but with humor. The following text was written for Lughnasadh 2001, the theme of which was the Bohemian mythical hero Bivoj. To me, the Celtic world, archaic thought, and distant memories generally are like a landmass that gradually rises above the sea and slowly grows grass and trees, in which birds build their nests.

*   *   *

I'm sitting on a train to České Budějovice and I think to myself, "For Christ's sake, *Carmen's blue-eyed love can read within the hearts of sorcerers*, but does she know what's going on in the kelp and in the roots of trees?" How do we find out about things we probably depend on—how is the forest doing, what does the soil have to say after a long winter, and how do the clouds above a power plant feel? After all, somewhere there the geochemical cycles of elements take place, where moisture is stored and the carbon dioxide in the air is broken down. Carmen can read inside the hearts of men and women, but outside of the human, *where the spell is still being cast and judgment is not yet cemented*, only the gods and the animals may read.

Vláda brought me the torso of the Salmon of Knowledge about a month ago so that I could check what kind of rock it was made of. When preparing their camp at Drábovna in Bohemian Paradise, some campers found a longish smoothed rock that was broken at both ends. Triangular markings are barely discernible on the weathered surface. We can say with near certainty that this strange torso is neither a forgery nor was it created in the Early Stone Age; judging by the smoothing, it dates from the time between the Neolithic and Aeneolithic periods. We know neither to whom this ancient object belonged, nor what it depicts. Nothing like it has been found here. There's something sacred about it, and most of all it resembles a fish. My guess is that when this *object* fulfilled its purpose, someone deliberately broke off its head and tail. Even the head of the Celtic hero from Žehrovice was intentionally destroyed and then piously buried.* It's an unknown heritage, a veiled legacy. It's probably better not to know and to guess than to look just once in a display case in a museum, see a specimen covered in dust, and read a caption about a cult object. *"Be wary of obvious clues, a trace of the obliterated is better."***

What is a miraculous fish good for? To deliver a message about the state of the world from places inaccessible to people and unvisited by the gods. The Welsh mythical figure Culhwch is connected to the mysterious fish of Llyn Alaw, similar to the Irish Salmon of Knowledge, who gained his abilities by eating nuts from nine hazel trees growing by a well at the bottom of the sea. What an image! A well at

---

* In 1943 the stone head of a Celtic hero was found close to a rectangular Celtic sanctuary. The head dates to the third century BC and is the most famous Celtic object in the National Museum in Prague.

** Passages in italics are quoted from Richard Weiner's book *Mezopotamie* (Mesopotamia) (Prague: Aventinum, 1930).

the bottom of the sea surrounded by miraculous trees! Many imagined wisdom or at least knowledge as a tepid, sparkling ocean of dark
waters, where we set aside reason and instead fumble about on instinct
and intuition. The deepest layers of groundwater and the highest layers of surface water are inaccessible to people living in between, and
thus they depend on friendly animals—prominent fish and birds.
People used to have the ability to secure for themselves the help and
partnership of animals. Something similar is true of gods as well; they
must seek the friendship and assistance of humans. The Celtic Pwyll
is asked to engage in single combat with Hafgan, Cú Chulainn fights
in place of beings from the underworld, and the Greek Heracles inter-
venes against the Giants. People need animals to go where they cannot, and from time to time the gods too need people to do what they
may not or cannot.

The balance of the world is also somehow dependent on
whether we will be able to communicate with animals at a critical moment and secure their assistance. I am very much against killing animals afflicted with foot-and-mouth disease; it's not fair to the animals
and in so doing we may be losing our claim to future communication
with them.

Bivoj carried the mighty wild boar to the sacred Vyšehrad. I
don't think he was trying to show off in front of the women, but either he wanted to demonstrate that he was as strong as the wild boar
or he brought the animal as a sacrifice. It's not a Rambo-style story,
but rather a scene from the magic world of powers, people, and gods.
Similarly, Heracles overpowered the Erymanthian Boar and brought
it alive to the sacred Mycenae. The boar, like all powerful beings, has
the ability to do great evil as well as great good. Diarmaid dies after
touching the poisoned bristles of the terrible boar of Beann Ghulban
in battle. A huge boar with a dazzling white coat lured Pryderi into
a trap in an enchanted castle. The destructive enchanted boar Twrch
Trwyth annihilates human settlements. The mythical boar is present

in two basic forms—either it is a symbol of bellicosity, as is the case in Slavic and Celtic mythology, or, conversely, it is a symbol of prosperity and good fortune. In this form it survives to this day as the good luck piglet.

In a normal Czech forest we often encounter soil rutted by wild boars. They are searching for food—larvae, concealed acorns, edible roots. They loosen the top layer of the soil so the seedlings of trees can penetrate it more easily. The boar means renewal of the forest, as though in his footsteps a green oak forest sprang up from the forgotten acorns. The boar signifies fertility and labor with the soil. In the Norse tradition it is similar to the sun, which opens and revitalizes the soil. The most congenial of the Norse gods, Freyr, received the iron boar Gullinbursti from the dwarves. His bristles gleam like the sun and he can race across the skies faster than a horse.

The older layer of Celtic and Norse mythology, and Czech fairy tales, is connected with mysterious ambidextrous animals, monsters and helpers. Their meaning has been lost beneath later layers of interpretation. Despite this, however, we can sense in it the reverberation of some ancient world, a world where humans and animals were not so divided from one another, their fates intertwined and the world they created a common space for the elements, forces, and creatures. The borders were permeable, and humans were not masters, but merely one of many parts of this world. I don't want to reminisce deeply and madly or explain vaguely. I used to read that one should *"rather cuddle a snake in one's breast than discover the truth."*

I recently attended a lecture on the sacred *hieros gamos* ritual at the Center for Theoretical Study. It's a thorny topic because the forces of this world that find one of their manifestations in the difference between a man and a woman defy description, and so it's easier to talk about sexuality in the vernacular of the pub. It's a very cheerful affair, unless one notices the great, powerful shadow of the aged deity in the background. I mused: what did the Celtic gods look like in the

Mesozoic? After all, they were here (at least the Old Ones) at the birth of this world. Long before people, the deeds of heroes, the guiles of tricksters, the loves of devoted and treacherous women. How do we appear to these gods? From their perspective, we have been here only for an imperceptible instant, or did they dream about us even before the first plants emerged from the ocean?

What did the Celtic gods look like before humans appeared? Were they small, radiant dinosaurs with large tusks and golden scales? Then my mythical world of human resemblances and familiar objects started to crumble . . . to be replaced by overlapping lights and shadows . . . terror entered with a supernatural calm. And in order to live, I hastily chased it all away and forgot about it.

Journey to India:
In Benares One Comes
to Understand That One
Was Born in Libeň

9

What seemed a utopia is approaching. India is within arm's reach. Everyone should travel there to visit the foundations of one's ancient civilizations, and to see problems greater than one's own. Years later I pick up the diary from my four-month journey, flip through the pages, and select a few contradictory observations. It's nice to be at home, but only away from it do we begin to understand where our home really is, as well as how small and limited it is. Only foreign lands give us the opportunity to return home.

* * *

Wiedner tells me, "Beware of Indian tolerance, it is so great as to be indifferent to others. Everyone has their fate, so why worry about others?" *Tolerance is a lack of love.* I'm reading Luis Bromfield's *Night in Bombay* and I'm thinking that Indian theology is blind. They investigated spiritual matters and concluded that they are immensely complicated, but the complexity tied their hands. They discovered remarkable things—humanities—and developed them to such a depth and breadth so as to become hopelessly lost within them.

Grotto in the Wallenstein Garden, Prague

*   *   *

India is so large that it cannot be described. But nor can one give up trying.

*   *   *

I meet a fastidious sadhu. He shows me how to manipulate kundalini and he requests my candy bar. I refuse to part with it, which visibly irritates him. He tries to punish me metaphysically. In the morning a native steals my flashlight, which was lying right next to my sleeping bag. I run after him, he drops it, and my friends scold me for not yelling "Go get 'em!" as we had agreed for such circumstances. Surrounded by locals, I'm writing in my diary in the courtyard of the police station in Varanasi. I'll probably start kicking their asses in a little while. A typical situation. I'm returning from the garden where Krishna danced. The monks are fat and look like criminals. No great sublimity, just stench, dirt, and dealing. The relationship to the gods: I give and you give too. They live a lot from the past here; the past is ground up and sold. Hinduism is also tolerant because it has so many strange deities: why enrage them?

*   *   *

The monsoon clings to us. It's our third day traveling through a flooded landscape where only the road embankment protrudes. I know already that if I were to write a book about India, it would be about the Grand Trunk Road along which Kim journeyed, about fish on the road, about inconsiderate drivers and that great turmoil where everyone is living amid the waters on one embankment. But then I realize I'm never going to write anything major about India; it's just between the two of us. And it can't be disclosed.

*   *   *

It's not a problem to run over a man, but it is a problem to drive into a cow. A small boy falls right under our wheels, Jarda slams

on the brakes, and the Liaz comes to a halt. We didn't kill him. Do
we even have the right to travel somewhere? I talk to the people and
look at folk woodcuts. "*To the last of the family, a Snake with a human
head appeared. . . .*" I think to myself: the same thing happened to the
woodcutter Chvala in Libín near Prachatice. Here you can find things
familiar from fairy tales, as if there had once been Hinduism in Bohemia. Here we live it; we talk about it in bedtime stories. It's a beautiful,
horrible religion: it's just a different prison, only uncommonly huge,
and so wide that it's not possible to reach its end.

*   *   *

I'm trying to arrange various permits to travel through Sikh
territory, but with the help of local bribed officials I'm done in a week.
In the evening I had a spat with my friends: they claimed they had
caught bedbugs from me. I don't feel like writing about the actual
traveler's experience, like discovering new caves, prospecting for gold,
about being chased up a tree by rhinos in the jungle, about how I accidentally stepped on a dead monk's skull in that creepy cave, or about
the evening scenery with a silent family incinerating a dead child by
the river. If this is about something, it's sickness, fear, and gradually
finding courage and curiosity. I feel really good in Surajkund by Delhi,
in an ancient proto-Hindu temple of the sun. It's like the Aeneolithic
settlement Zámka near Prague—did Erben and Božena Němcová
possibly write from this world?

*   *   *

I'm reading the texts of the Gelug-pa: *Compassion is necessary
at the beginning, compassion is necessary in the middle, compassion is
necessary at the end.* I think to myself that the Tibetans made two mistakes—they approached emotions rationally, and they saw compassion
only as a means to achieve enlightenment. Their culture went to hell
once they started to conceive of compassion as a means to an end. Then
I sleep for a long time and think about the explosions of hatred that

sometimes break out in Indian cities—a quarrel at the barber shop engulfed an entire neighborhood and resulted in sixteen deaths, I read in the paper. But then I immediately realize that I could also say a lot of bad things about my own culture. I listen to a Polish mountaineer talking about the situation after Indira Gandhi's assassination. People chased Sikhs, mostly drivers, poured gasoline over them, and set them on fire. There were even children among the victims. According to official statistics, there were two thousand deaths and during the initial days the police just looked on. I somehow incorporate this into my image of India to give it depth and height. It's a mosaic of words and images, and among them amazement and disgust.

*   *   *

Later I'm astonished in the library in Delhi and read on and on: "Visualizing without Sunyata is dangerous. It accumulates fixed ground for the ego." But I also recall Kabir: "I laugh when I hear that the fish in the water is thirsty."

*   *   *

Once the monks of Sera caught the Mad Yogi of Bhutan and built a stupa over him so that he could not make mischief. They buried him alive. Some time later, the prior ran into him in the streets of Lhasa. The Mad Yogi told him that he couldn't go up and so he had gone down to hell, which had been full of his monks; there was only one place left—and that was for you, oh prior! Then he disappeared.

*   *   *

In front of a Buddha statue in the Gupta style, I repeat its components: the highest vision—drishti; form—rupa; emotion—bhava; grace and charm—lavanya; and resemblance of the ideal—sadrishia. It is the male counterpart to the beautiful Madonna in southern Bohemia, and both will be my lifelong companions.

　*　*　*

We crossed the Indus and ran over a dog. Another month of travel and adventure. At home, and attending the birthday celebration of his majesty the king of Nepal. On the wall there's a Gobelin tapestry with the inscription "Life was a gift I could not bear whenever I was alone." Mr. Vavroušek from the long-ago Lambaréné expedition looks at me, "We did not just want to go abroad, we wanted to espouse a certain idea. It has marked my entire life."

　*　*　*

I selected these notes from my diaries of a four-month truck journey to the Himalayas, where we partially discovered and mapped the second largest system of caves on the Indian subcontinent in Cobhar Gorge south of Kathmandu (today this work has been surpassed by others). I didn't write about any adventures, because they're all quite similar and rather boring (I almost died there). When I returned, I finally began to prefer my own culture and I also chose the place I call home. It's the Libeň* district of Prague. It took me thirty years to begin to understand where I belong.

Božena Němcová's Journey to India: You Will Find Babička in Dobšiná

If I may speak personally, I must say that what most intrigued me in India was encountering some of the deeper roots of my own Indo-European civilization. The caste system prescribes how roles and occupations are to be inherited. In some families, the occupation of, for example, a potter is something that spans dozens of generations without interruption. It's a great experience to see a ceramist using a stick

---

* Libeň is the part of Prague which is associated with the life of Czech writer Bohumil Hrabal. When I reached middle age, I chose it as my birthplace.

to set his lathe in motion like a gigantic flywheel and quickly throw
a vessel. In Europe a similar technology is known from archeological
research, but even the Celts were able to construct a more modern
treadle wheel or kick wheel. The continuity of tradition, storytelling,
sacrificing to local gods, the contact with water and fire has equally
ancient roots. In India one finds oneself in a forgotten world—as if in
a fairy tale—of one's childhood and the dawn of Europe. This motif is
clearly discernible in the whole range of classical English literature on
the "journey to India."

The Czech view of Slovakia also frequently has similar romantic, folkloric, and antiquarian features of longing for a landscape still
inhabited by something that we in Bohemia have lost due to progress
and migration to cities. I know several secrets of the Slovak regions
and I know that in Silica in the Slovak Karst, the village sings a secret
song no one else may know. I talk to people who tell me only after
many years of acquaintance about a shepherd's magic and sorcery to
gain a love. Even the Slovak poet Štefan Žáry saw a snake with a crown
near Poniky. People tell me of a dancing broom in the forest above
Dobšiná as though it were a great secret. Occasionally, something of
India touches me in Slovakia's current, post-postmodern mountains
and villages, but it's extremely difficult to prove such influences. Many
of my acquaintances have been changed by a journey to India, but
without being able to express what this change consisted of. Is it perhaps some hard-to-appreciate expansion and deepening of the soul,
some personal growth that bears deep and invisible fruit?

I can imagine that if Božena Němcová* had lived in Victorian
England, she might have set her stories and folkloric observations in, say,
Dharamsala. In the small proportions of our country, however, Slova-
kia played a similar role (fortunately for both nations). It is well known

---

* Božena Němcová (1820–1862) was a Czech female writer and a founding figure of
Czech prose. She is one of only a very few classic authors who are still loved by the nation
in spite of school education.

Old monastery, Klášter

that Božena Němcová undertook four journeys to Slovakia between 1851 and 1855. The influence of the Slovak people and wilderness on her literary work has been analyzed many times. Less is known about her extensive study of Slovak realia, which was to lead to an expansive work on Slovak ethnography. She even considered a plan for an encyclopedia, on which Jan Krejčí was to participate. Krejčí's thousand-page *Geologie čili nauka o útvarech zemských se zvláštním ohledem na krajiny československé* (Geology or the science of the forms of the earth with special respect to the Czechoslovak landscapes; Prague, 1877) is considered a seminal work of Czech geology, and it is an open question whether the Slovak part wasn't originally inspired by Němcová. It has been claimed that in autumn 1859 the publisher Augusta promised to take up the Slovak encyclopedia project, and that he would sponsor an excursion to Slovakia by the authors. The plan was abandoned, however, because of financial difficulties. Thus of Němcová's great literary plans, "only" the book of Slovak fairy tales materialized. Under different circumstances and in a wealthier milieu, she might have become the main editor of a basic encyclopedia of Slovak natural and cultural anthropology. Instead of one large monograph, Němcová published a number of short essays that she had authored or, more frequently, edited. I consider the following to be her fundamental contributions: "Obrazy ze života Slováků" (Images from the life of Slovaks; 1858), "Obrazy ze života slovenského" (Images from Slovak life; 1859), "Kraje a lesy na Zvolensku" (Landscapes in the Zvolen region; 1859), "Uherské město Ďarmoty" (The Hungarian town of Ďarmoty; 1858), and "Slovenské starožitnosti" (Slovak antiques; 1858). In these works, she makes a number of unexpected observations about the formation of calcite through the escape of carbon dioxide from a solution, the discovery of crystallized celestine in Špania Dolina, and karst hydrology. In her time, the worlds of art and science were still inseparably linked.

    I know I'm walking on thin ice when I rely on my own time-honored, enchanted experience as a wayfarer and natural scientist to whom Slovakia has given something that Bohemia cannot (except for extraordinary places like Josef Váchal's Šumava).* It's a sort of hard-to-explain contact with aspects of life—forests, rocks, and subterranean streams, but also folktales that bring one into an archaic but still living world of legends and rural sorcery. We'll never know what the Slovak experience meant to Němcová, and I doubt even she would know fully. Nonetheless, let's try to suggest that the mountains and forests of Slovakia opened up a new realm of perception for her. I can't find the right words, but people who have had the same experience know what I'm trying to say.

I'm astonished by the titles of her works: "Obrazy ze života slovenského" (Images from Slovak life), "Obrazy ze života Slováků" (Images from the life of Slovaks), and naturally also the subtitle of *Babička* (The grandmother; 1855): "Obrazy venkovského života" (Images of rural life). All these "works as images" were created during a period corresponding roughly to her stays in Slovakia. Similar titles and descriptions of folk customs in *Babička* suggest a deeper kinship of themes, and it is possible that the Slovak and rural images form one indivisible experiential whole. It may be that the two themes influenced each other, and without this Slovak inspiration there may have been no Czech *Babička*. The Slovak sketches are diaries of cultural anthropology of sorts, a kind of realization of the point of departure and method. *Babička* is not only a literature of emotion and childhood, it is also connected to omnipresent nature and the archaic mind of the folktale. Myth, the elements, and feeling connected into a single world thus form a triad that expressed an important part of the national spirit, and later flowed into it.

*   *   *

* Josef Váchal (1884–1969), a Czech artist and writer, was a master of colored woodcuts and composed sarcastic books about ghosts, planets, and mystics. In the Czech tradition he is sometimes compared to William Blake.

This morning I returned from Slovakia. Peter Holúbek showed me a mysterious cave called Zápolná that in all likelihood connects the Biely Váh and Čierny Váh Rivers underground. He told me about how in a cave in the Demänová slopes, which is also a bears' den, they found a hissing mushroom. He told me about the pains they took to identify it and the accompanying skepticism. I'm not concerned with the case of the "singing mushroom," but rather with the fact that such things continue to happen in Slovakia. The "defolklorized" Czech mushroom would most likely not utter a peep. Czech legends are folktales or reading for children, not stories of life. If you look at some of the numerous books of Slovak legends published by Matica sloven-ská, however, you will understand just from the illustrations that the strange magic that lives in the mountains and forests of Slovakia lives in the people as well. Why should we study mythology if we can live it? The invisible Slovak inspiration of the "world of the recent distant past" feeds not only a part of Czech culture but also a certain part of our forgotten ties to the land that nourished us, to the mountains, and to the forests. How shall we thank you, Slovakia?

It's a long story involving several dates, which I normally don't like because they remind me of history lessons at school. But I have to mention them to make clear that, in order to be able to have the right feelings in our souls, we need physical contact with objects and places. One of the implications of this slightly hagiographic story for me is quite practical: it is necessary to take care of the landscape, environment, and monuments on a completely ordinary, physical level. It really is that simple.

*   *   *

Intolerant, restless, and unsuccessful—this is how we might describe the character of St. Adalbert, but taking into account the fact that applying our metric of tolerance to circumstances where the rivalry of two political groups leads to the slaughter of an entire lineage, where restlessness is a sign of a true search, and where success is measured mainly in relation to eternity, this is equally as misleading as current attempts to establish Adalbert as a proponent of Europeanism. Although he was a friend of German emperors, lived as a monk in Italy, confirmed Stephen, the future king of Hungary, and brought Western values to the East Prussians, his idea of Europe as a single whole, interconnected by shared values, was essentially a fiasco and an example

not worth following, then or now. Europe has always been more of a "concert of nations and regions" than a sort of "United States of Europe," and its civilization is more of a culture of individualities that can reach agreement among each other than a set of uniform rules of a huge empire. This is evidenced by the fragmentation of European states into smaller or larger regions whenever circumstances have allowed. Even our recent history attests to this.

In the consciousness of the people, Adalbert—frequently mentioned and all too often forgotten—is rather revered than loved. In baroque legends he is connected either with the elements—plants and springs—or with punishments for blasphemers and churls. In paintings and sculptures he appears rather "in company" with St. Wenceslaus, and usually isn't doing anything; he doesn't give anything out, rescue those in need, or perform miracles. One of the major reasons for this neglect is undoubtedly connected with his relics; as we shall see, they were hidden so well that the people of the baroque era lacked the kind of contact from which legends are born.

His life was complicated, and the restlessness of his journeys reminds me of Jack Kerouac's characters in *On the Road*. He was born in unsettled times, when the Czech state and the Czech nation were taking shape. His father, Slavník, ruled half of Bohemia, from Netolice to Kłodzko in Poland. They say "if" is unscientific, but in those times it was truly unclear whether the capital of the kingdom might not be Kouřim, and its founder might not be a mythical plowman of the Slavník dynasty.* The conflict was also accentuated by the fact that the Slavníks focused more on Saxony, whereas the Přemyslids directed their attention toward strengthening their ties with Bavaria. By accepting the bishop's office in the Přemyslid principality, Adalbert became a partial vassal. He was constantly forced to balance the inter-

* Czech legendary history begins with Přemysl the Plowman, who seems to be a mythical king plowing a furrow during spring fertility rites. It is likely that this custom was widespread among other tribes and clans in these times.

🜎 *Loretta Chapel with century plant, Římov, Bohemia*

ests of the church and strong ties to the opposing political power with the interests of the principality.

Even his death as a martyr not far from what later became a significant Russian military base—modern-day Kaliningrad (founded by Ottokar II of Bohemia in 1255 in Adalbert's honor)—speaks volumes. The Prussians asked him to leave. They couldn't risk that an unfamiliar stranger in odd dress might undermine their faith in the local gods, which—as every Prussian well knew—would cause the fields to go barren and the children to die of hunger. They were willing to treat him respectfully, but Adalbert, who, it turns out, had feared suffering his entire life, decided not to back down. But nor could the Prussians suffer the subversion of their principality, and so the story ended, to the satisfaction of both parties, in Adalbert's death. For a time the Prussians managed to protect their good old values, and the Czechs and Poles gained a martyr who united them, at least when they weren't bickering over his relics. In the nineteenth century even the Slovaks adopted Adalbert for lack of enough of their own saints, and the emigrants exported him to America, but that is the story of the cult of Adalbert.

It was extremely important for a medieval kingdom to have its own domestic saints; it was something like a Nobel Prize, a gold medal in hockey, or membership in the European Union. It showed that a country was a full-fledged member of the community. A saint was not an abstract concept of morals and theology, but had to be quite physically present in the form of relics. If an Orthodox priest visits Prague today and searches for the relics of Procopius, Ludmila, or Adalbert, he is flabbergasted by the negligible respect afforded to the bones of the saints, which aren't of much interest to anyone—even to believers.

In the Middle Ages, however, things were different. When Bretislaus I plundered the golden treasure of the cathedral in Gniezno with the help of Severus in 1039, he couldn't resist taking the relics of

St. Adalbert, Radim Gaudentius, and the Five Holy Brothers. Had he been forced to choose, he would rather have parted with the gold than the bones of the saints. What was from the Polish point of view a contemptible robbery became for the Kingdom of Bohemia a ceremonial relocation of the relics, celebrated each year on August 25. The theft was excused in a complicated way in the form of St. Adalbert's consent, which was given only if Bretislaus's army would renounce its pagan sins.

The entire twelfth century witnessed a growing reverence toward Adalbert, which even spread to the neighbors of the Kingdom of Bohemia. Otto of Bamberg founded a church consecrated to St. Adalbert in Pomerania in 1125. The following year, St. Adalbert's standard was affixed to St. Wenceslaus's pike during the Battle of Chlumec, and when it ended in victory, no one doubted Adalbert's power (Wenceslaus's was clear from the outset). The chivalrous thirteenth century naturally favored Wenceslaus, but Adalbert established himself as his poor and intellectual complement. It was a most suitable and desirable combination, as the medieval world was dominated by the duality of worldly and spiritual power. This once inconvenient Slavník now became quite useful to the Přemyslids.

An exceptional devotee was John IV of Dražice, who commissioned a new and uncommonly beautiful tombstone of silver and gold for Adalbert's grave. His attachment is understandable—he, too, was a bishop and lived in uncertain political circumstances. Just thirteen years later the indebted John of Bohemia ordered excavations in the vicinity of the tombstone and removed statues made of precious metals from the grave of St. Wenceslaus. The indignation was tremendous. (I wouldn't be surprised if the people of Prague were making comments like: "Don't be surprised that things turned out so disgracefully at Crécy.") And thus the people welcomed all the more Charles IV's plan to build a spectacular new cathedral at Prague Castle where the relics of both national saints might be displayed. In 1346, Charles IV personally inspected Adalbert's relics in the presence of Ernest of Pardubice. They were then wrapped and in 1396, when construction of St. Vitus Cathedral had progressed sufficiently, they were interred in the middle of the church. They were deposited so thoroughly that they would never again play a significant role in Czech history.

The precise location of Adalbert's relics in the cathedral changed several times. An important role was played here by a huge fire in 1541 that started on Pětikostelní Square in a house known as Bašta. Part of the Lesser Town fell victim to it, and it also burned one tower of St. Vitus Cathedral at the castle. The fire spread from the tower to the western part of the church, provisionally roofed with shingles, and Adalbert's white marble tombstone was cracked badly from the heat. Between 1421 and 1561, the office of the Prague archbishop was vacant, and thus it was several years before Ferdinand I started the reconstruction. The cathedral was shortened and closed off by a wall, which was later decorated with scenes from the life of St. John of Nepomuk. This modification, however, placed Adalbert's tomb outside the church. A small chapel was built above it in 1576, which was expanded in 1673. One of the reasons for its expansion was the fact that the cathedral's complete interior was destroyed during the iconoclastic uprisings of 1619, although the tombs of St. Wenceslaus and St. Adalbert remained untouched.

By the beginning of March 1880, construction of St. Vitus Cathedral had progressed to such an extent that on March 8 workers began carrying furniture and the little organ out of the St. Adalbert Chapel. Despite written records, however, it was not clear whether Adalbert's relics were still inside. Bishop Karel Průcha asked architect Josef Mocker for help. It was known that the chapel had a two-part altar. Its upper wooden part had contained a picture of the Mother of God, brought from the chapel at Bruska. The extended lower part of the altar consisted of a stone landing which continued in a form resembling a wooden coffin that was thought to be Adalbert's. For the Feast of St. Adalbert, the altar used to be adorned and the saint's bust, which held smaller relics and a little cross allegedly having belonged to him, was displayed.

Workers in the empty chapel proceeded to tear down the catafalque, but to the disappointment of all present it was empty. When the wooden trunk was dismantled, however, a red marble slab six centimeters thick was revealed. It bore the inscription *Renovatum anno 1717*. Again there was optimism, as it was expected with near certainty that the relics would be found beneath the slab. Instead, there was a small lined chest containing a lead box about four centimeters in length. Canon Bernard took it out and checked the seal attached to a ribbon tied around the box. The tassel disintegrated, however, with the first touch. Inside, there was a faded paper document certifying authenticity. It was impossible to read the inscription, however, even with the help of a magnifying glass, and the sheet fell apart as well. Fortunately, there were bone fragments at the bottom of the box labeled as relics of the Holy Five Brothers. The seal belonged to Prague archbishop Jan Lohelius (1612–1622), who reconsecrated the entire cathedral in the turbulent year 1621 after the flight of the Winter King, Frederick V, elector palatine, and placed a new relic chest in the altar.

Further excavations revealed slabs of white marble, visibly damaged by the fire of 1541. The digging continued with great care, but again, nothing was found. Only at floor level did the workers discover some six long sandstone slabs resembling other entrances to tombs. The anticipation grew. One of the workers lifted the outer stone, revealing an empty space and a sort of coffin. They immediately sent for the suffragan bishop, who ordered the slab returned to its original position and sealed it.

On March 15 at 2 P.M. a committee of church dignitaries, archeologists, and other notable figures convened. In the end even Baron

Weber arrived, accompanied by high-ranking officers.* The suffragan bishop gave a factual summary of the situation, and explained why the chapel was being torn down and what had been found thus far. He pointed to the sealed stone and pronounced that no one had yet looked in the tomb. The archbishop bid the others to pious attention and regretted that Professor Václav Vladivoj Tomek** dwelled outside of Prague. Then they set to work.

Not half an hour later it was clear that the tomb held an ancient reliquary resembling in its shape that of St. Wolfgang of Regensburg, who had supported the establishment of the Prague bishopric and was therefore always revered in Bohemia. The tomb's profile had dimensions of 302 × 72.5 centimeters and the reliquary's dimensions were 112 × 38 × 32 centimeters. At about one-quarter of the tomb's length there was a low sandstone wall, behind which lay pieces of rotten wood, possibly the remnants of old reliquaries.

Adalbert's reliquary was made of wood covered with lead plates. The workers carefully removed the lid and revealed to eager eyes a longish lead chest tied with a ribbon and sealed with an elongated seal in ancient script. On top of the chest lay a lead plate with a Latin inscription. Canon Bernard placed it on a prepared table. A witness to this event wrote, "It cannot easily be described what eagerness and anticipation ruled the moment." In the meantime, Professor Josef Emler deciphered the inscription and read aloud, "Capsa cum corpora seu reliquiis s. Adalberti episcopi et martyris." It was clear that Adalbert's relics were inside, and "Deo gratias!" spontaneously resounded, and great joy shone in the eyes of all present.

And then a new and unexpected surprise followed. The following words were deciphered from the elongated seal: "Arnestus ar-

---

* The presence of a military leader and prominent officers was needed to corroborate the verification, as in these times one could not question an officer's statement.
** Václav Vladivoj Tomek (1818–1905) was a Czech historian famous for his twelve-volume history of Prague.

🌿 *Tree and roots, southern Bohemia*

chiepiscopus pragensis," that is, Ernest, archbishop of Prague. It was almost a double miracle, since Ernest himself enjoyed the reputation of a saint. Canon Bernard opened the chest, in which he finally found bones wrapped in a gray silk veil. On the cloth lay a third plate with an inscription confirming that the relics belonged to other saints as well. Even greater joy ensued.

They then wrapped up the chest again. The archbishop took the crosier and the miter. The canons placed the reliquary on a bier and carried it out of the chapel. At that particular moment the bells in the belfry of St. Vitus Cathedral began to ring, which caused no small sensation. In front of the chapel stood the lower clergy and curious onlookers. Many of them fell to their knees and intoned a song perhaps arranged by St. Adalbert himself: "Hospodine pomiluj nás" (Lord have mercy upon us). Others cried and could not sing for their tears. Everyone was made aware of just how deeply the Czech people revered the relics, even nonbelievers. The procession then deposited the reliquary in the chapel opposite the tombstone of John of Nepomuk, where Deacon Carolus Franciscus Průcha had had the space modified for relics collected in particular by Charles IV. After the ceremonial entombment the committee retired to decipher the lead plates and to record the event. Mocker received the order to preserve the tomb for future entombments and the bishop commissioned another lead plate—a fourth.

The find deeply moved the people of Prague while at the same time enraging the Poles, who were already in possession of the genuine skull of St. Adalbert. The disputes continued for the next twenty years, and Mikoláš Aleš, for example, commented on them by means of a drawing that depicts St. Adalbert asking God where his genuine skull was. The Lord replies that not even he can answer the question and refers Adalbert to a decision of the church consistory.

In Bohuslav Martinů's opera *The Greek Passion*, Fotis, priest of the Greek exiles from Turkey, says: "Daughter of the Almighty, great stone! And thou water, that knowest no end and springest from the rock to quench the thirst of the deer and the falcon. And thou, fire, who sleepest in the wood and waitest for man to awaken thee. Blessed be the hour of our meeting. We are men, hunted by wild men, wild, sorrowful souls. *We bring the bones of our fathers.*" And the chorus answers: "The bones of our fathers. . . . May we take root among these rocks and stones. Hear us, Lord."

In the second half of the nineteenth century, in the age of Jules Verne's hopes, the Eiffel Tower, and superphosphate, the pressure of steam in the boiler of a mighty machine, iron and rivets, or the arch span of the railway bridge built forty-eight meters above the Thaya River in 1871 became the most exciting topics of conversation. A second Iron Age ensued, whose children were the furnaces of Kladno, an iron ore refinery in Ejpovice, and a world in which the bones of ancestors—for protection from sorrowful souls and as a means of connecting with the earth—ceased to be interesting. Bolts and rivets, ore and coal, *Robur the Conqueror* and Anton Gareis's lithographs of coffins with relics hastily removed from the walls,* cremations, not understanding Felix Jenewein's art** and disputes about who had the more genuine skull of St. Adalbert. And gradually half-forgotten relics, abandoned Rain Madonnas, and adoration statues become food for art historians. Only the Infant Jesus of Prague, the Palladium of Bohemia in Boleslav, and the Madonna of Svatá hora remain, but more as historical monuments than as vessels of divine grace.

Today we don't know what to do with the bones. It's impossible to return to the faith of our fathers; we have moved on and know very well how uncertain authenticity may be. But I also see children looking at skeletons in the archaeological section. I show American

* The motif of death was common in the Czech lands from baroque times to about 1850, but then faded with nineteenth-century industrialization and almost disappeared with twentieth-century globalization.
** Felix Jenewein (1857–1905) was a Czech religious artist who often painted motifs of plagues, decaying corpses, and scenes from Czech history.

students around in Czech ossuaries and I watch their distrustful, but curious looks, their fascination with ephemerality. "*These bones, this is us? This dust?* The health department back home wouldn't allow this." The bones of our ancestors send us a clear indication that we will once again become one with the soil and the earth, and that this isn't anything terrible. The saints' bones carry an even deeper message: soil, grain, and death are simple and natural things, but sacredness is here, too, and a narrow gate leads to a place where not even Dr. Moody has set foot. *The breath of bones*, intimate and sacred. It cannot be described and it's indecent to intrude upon it.

The breath of bones. I heard about the case of a man who had access to various relics thanks to his research. From time to time he would break off or cut off a piece and began collecting them as curiosities, the way other people collect stamps. For years he stored them in boxes; sometimes he would take them in his hand and wipe off the dust. Ten years passed, and he started looking for a goldsmith who would make him a relic cross. But such things must be stored with dignity and serve everyone! He knew then as he knows now that he will return them to a church one day. It could have been quite a sacrilege, but it was derailed thanks to the breath of the bones.

I don't advocate the cult of relics, which is something different from the cult of the saints. I don't believe in the historical authenticity of many of them. They may not be authentic, but I have no doubt about their sincerity. They breathe strength as well as helplessness. Is it just a reminder of death? Or a hint that it can be transcended? I don't know how to approach them and I have no suggestions for others. *The Story of St. Adalbert's bones demonstrates one important thing: without relics, adoration objects, and sacred places, without such grounding in the material sphere, a cult, emotion, or poetic image often becomes a mere abstract construction.* Since the fourteenth century, when his relics disappeared, Adalbert has been revered, but not loved. It is as though his spirit was not present in Bohemia; he is a saint in company and has the slightly uncomfortable reputation of a moralist, unlike Nepomuk or Wenceslaus.

Adalbert Breaks His Staff for a Second Time

The story does not end here. You may have noticed that almost everything in this book actually took place in some way; there are notes from negotiations, meetings, field trips, and conversations by the fire late at night. Records of signs constitute a favorite motif of medieval and baroque literature. Allow me to continue this abandoned tradition. At the beginning of February 2002 some thirty people gathered in St. Vitus Cathedral to watch Zdeněk Neubauer* deposit a newly fabricated crosier of St. Adalbert containing his relics on the altar in the chapel across from the tomb of St. John of Nepomuk. The St. Wenceslaus Crown belongs to St. Wenceslaus and was placed on his skull; he only lends it to the king of Bohemia. If Charles IV restored the St. Wenceslaus Crown (he certainly had his advisers), it was most likely not a collective foundation but Václav Havel himself who restored St. Adalbert's crosier. The trouble with symbols is that if they are genuine, then they are not mere toys in our hands, and their actions can escape our will. The granodiorite obelisk in the Third Courtyard of Prague Castle was to symbolize the unity of the Czech nation, but it broke during transport and its smaller pieces were used to make curbstones. The rest stands there like a stela on the grave of an unknown magnate. This is how symbols behave.

Four years ago the Vize Foundation was established, which not only organizes its famous forums but also awards a prize to a deserving researcher each year. In the first year, this was given to Karl

---

* Zdeněk Neubauer is a contemporary Czech philosopher who is understood by few, but these few—among them myself and, more important, Václav Havel—feel they have been profoundly changed by him.

Pribram, whose grandfather was Franz Kafka's emplo_
ated a holographic model of the human brain. In th_
was conferred on Umberto Eco, a writer and medie_
the third year the recipient was an eccentric professo_
Street of small stature named Zdeněk Neubauer, a forgotten local genius who had influenced and inspired generations of friends and students. He was the last holder of the crosier. Zdeněk experiences and
identifies with everything to such a degree that it becomes an ideal, be
it St. Francis or a hobbit from the Shire. And so it came to pass that
one day before handing over the crosier, he heard something crash in
his closet but paid no attention to it, thinking a picture had fallen. A
few hours before the handover of the lightweight metal crosier was to
take place, he discovered that this sacred symbol was in two pieces! It
was as though the St. Wenceslaus Crown had fallen and a couple of
stones had broken off. A terrible situation.

We met in front of the cathedral. I sat to one side, but I sensed
a certain restlessness. Then various rationalizations began to emerge,
such as it was a good symbol, just like in *The Lord of the Rings*. We
entered. I accidentally took Zdeněk's briefcase containing his speech,
leaned on a pillar, and took in the cathedral with that Kafkaesque
feeling from *The Trial* that we are all guilty. Václav Havel read an excerpt from Cosmas's *Chronicle of Bohemia*,* Zdeněk gave thanks for
the crosier, and Michal Jůza deposited it on the altar. Tomáš Halík**
reviewed the events of Adalbert's life, including the part where he returns to Bohemia, breaks his staff over the nation, and leaves to die
at the hands of the Prussians. When the Franconians broke a staff, it
meant a disengagement from society: I am no longer yours; we share
neither the same destiny nor the same obligations.

---

* Cosmas (c. 1045–1125) was a priest, writer, and historian, and is the author of the first
Bohemian chronicle.
** Tomáš Halík (b. 1948) is a Czech public intellectual, a Roman Catholic priest, and the
author of several popular books about religion and the human condition.

Understandably, the endings of such stories are left open; they are still maturing. This is what happened in the triad of Power (Havel)—Faith (Halík)—Wisdom (Neubauer); if anything unusual occurs in a cathedral, it's usually something that concerns the entire community. We sometimes laughed, downplayed the situation, but it really did seem as though Adalbert had broken with the Czech nation for a second time. It actually unnerved me quite a bit. Or rather, it actually unnerves me quite a bit. I'm not trying to convince you and I don't insist that you believe it. All my life I have encountered stories that could have taken place in Gothic or baroque times, or even earlier. For me it's not history, but a continuation of the current of life. I was there; I'm giving an account of it and I'm waiting. But actually it's so pathetic and elegant that one must ask: Am I not imagining this? What if the crosier was just a piece of junk, like so many other things in this kingdom?

The Czech philosopher Jan Sokol later sent me a letter in which he expanded on this ancient living memory and the bones of ancestors:

> I began to understand the entombed bones of ancestors
> a bit only after having read Fustel de Coulanges,* when I
> verified in places he cites that it is indeed a constant, at least
> of staid cultures.
>
> My interpretation is quite simple: religion (like
> philosophy) begins with astonishment over what we have
> in this world, but it takes it one step further. It does not ask,
> "how come there is something and not nothing," but instead

---

* The work in question is the remarkable book *The Ancient City* by Fustel de Coulanges (first published in 1864). The feelings of repeated events and of the interconnections in the world are expressed well in R. H. Benson's book *The Light Invisible* (Prague, 1930, 1998), in the essays of W. B. Yeats, and also, e.g., in Dylan Thomas's volume of poetry *Deaths and Entrances* (1946; see "The Conversation of Prayer").

poses a more practical question: "to whom do we owe it and who therefore can also help avoid losing it?" The cult and the rite are thus not just "self-expression of the community" as Durkheim thought, but an attempt to respond to what we know we have received and continue to receive. Individual religions differ only in who the recipient of this care and gratitude is: the forest, the sea, the totem animal, and especially our ancestors—in short, to those from whom we received life (and our trade or livelihood). They are also most likely competent to help us preserve it.

Since then I've been amazed time and again at how omnipresent and alive this fundamental idea is (thinly veiled) in the Christian cult, even when "religion" has vanished. At the Olšany Cemetery, the Prague bourgeoisie does the same things as our ancestors did a thousand years ago, but they don't know it. (Fustel draws attention to the ancient phrase "Here rests X.Y.," for which there is no theological explanation.) At the church door we always reach for the holy water in the stoup, and above the altar (the tomb of our ancestor) the eternal light, ancient Hestia, glimmers.

The interesting thing about visions is that we gain information about the appearance of something that usually looks completely different. Visions speak to us in an allegorical tongue and if they are true, it is usually a truth hidden behind an image, rather than the truth of an image. There are people who long for visions, and thus wake from their slumber, usually to their own detriment, because such visions generally bring deep experiences and deep confusion. There are people who gain real insight into this world that cannot be held or taken hold of for long, and if they lose this ability, their mind produces gibberish with some true elements of their past visionary glory. Often, however, they just copy and deconstruct their own thoughts. Otokar Březina* wrote his oeuvre in six years and then was disciplined enough to keep silent. There are also delusional visions that come from a playful and sometimes slightly malicious world, and which take on random shapes. They emerge through some mysterious friction on the border of dragons' veins and the usual geological substrate, or in places where strong feelings collide. Such visions are not to be interpreted in terms of reason, but rather using the metric of a wavering line or *melos domos*,

---

* Otokar Březina (1868–1929) was a symbolist poet who wrote his entire poetic oeuvre within six years and then chose to remain silent. He was one of the most profound spirits of the entire European poetic tradition on the order of magnitude of William Blake.

the rising path of a melody. I won't talk about them and I'll also avoid heights where I cannot see.

I'm more interested in a standard central Bohemian vision, which is experienced by some one-fifth of the population during their lives, according to statistics, and which forms the basis of folktales. It involves normal individuals who are not particularly gifted in any way. It often takes place in a natural setting or near death. Sometimes it changes people's lives, such as when one of my colleagues encountered a floating muscular forearm in the opal mines in Dubník near Prešov. Today we know that in the sense-deprived underground, parts of human bodies, usually hands, are rarely but regularly seen to float. But for my colleague, this experience will forever be a turning point in his errant consumer reality. Since then, the focus of his attention has shifted inward.

I recorded both the following stories from authentic accounts and I am leaving them in the first person. Unlike in folktales, I emphasize the vision's meaning rather than what it looked like. Many visionaries describe their visions to distinguish themselves from the crowd, because a vision is exclusive and not everyone has access to it. I have chosen the opposite approach, which is control of the interpretation, because everybody is sensible, even if few of us have "second sight."

An Indignant Young Man Walks to a Menhir

In Ládevská Street in the Chabry neighborhood of northern Prague there's a squat black quartzite stone that was brought here from Ládví, which lies about a kilometer away. In the yard of one family house lies its prostrate little brother. This tends to happen to upright stones—if they cannot be broken up or moved, one just digs a hole to bury them in. This was even the fate of some of the "menhirs" of the Kounov Alignments. Occasionally someone comes up with the

Moss-covered rock, southern Bohemia

idea of digging them out, but so far this has never materialized. The actual story is as simple as a folktale:

When I returned from my travels I learned that my friend was suffering from an illness that had nearly cost him his life. It was most probably caused by special exercises, during which he activated channels around the heart region and tried to enter into contact with the state of Bodhi. The result was lamentable, and even when my friend recovered, we never again found the path to one another. Because his concept of spirituality nearly cost him his life, his treatment went in the opposite direction. He started earning money and making up for years of asceticism. I was resentful, because I believed—as Aristotle did—that one has only one close friend for one's entire life. It was a real loss for me, and I felt disgust or even hatred toward all those forces between heaven and earth.

Into this disposition came the autumn equinox, and I felt annoyed and a little vindictive. Late one evening I set out for the menhir in Chabry so as to reach it at midnight. I set out from the end of the tram line in Ďáblice. Just the name—"devil's village"! The night was dark and I was full of spite. At the last moment I noticed the high cliff wall of a surface mine, from which I had almost fallen. A spell of fear. Then I realized I had to change my attitude, that something about me was not right, and I approached the menhir very circumspectly. There was still some time before midnight, so I propped myself up against the stone and fell asleep. I was cold. I was half-sleeping, then half-awake. And so in my half-waking state, careworn as a Native American on a vision quest, I saw white beings. They were women in white robes, moving as if they were dancing. I was suddenly

in the distant past. The spite suddenly vanished, lifted like
the curtain in a theater. I was overcome by a feeling of peace
and reconciliation that came not from the strangeness of
the experience, but from its contents—the experience that
in this country on this earth there has always been faith in
something very good. The local people have always watched
over the spark of the divine by their own means. Gratitude
toward old men of various confessions. And also a smile, that
on the outskirts of Prague fairies still dance.

As the one who recorded this story, I can say that the image of
fairies has faded over time, but not the experience. The person concerned changed his attitude toward the world and became more open
to the side roads of his own soul. Of course the story continues, not
only with the adventures of a wayfaring druid and a witch, but also
in an insistent letter by Kateřina N. about the sorrow of small stones.
Even so, I have already said more than I intended.

The Dragon of Tetín

I remember Josef Chvala* from Prachatice. During the First
Czechoslovak Republic he traveled the world with a circus, just like
his friends from Stachy who became famous thanks to Eduard Bass's
novel about the Humberto Circus. He was discharged from the
Wehrmacht for stupidity. He worked in the forest, and never really
learned to speak Czech. Once he went to Libín, met a snake with a
human head, and talked with it, which changed his life. His neighbors
thought he was a crackpot and the folklorists made a fine story of it.
Please show me a fine story that changes a person! At that point he

---

* Josef Chvala (Chwala, 1906–1985) was a woodcutter and folk carver from Prachatice,
a simple fool of God and forest beings.

had already become a bit of a celebrity, because he was now a much sought after folk woodcutter. At home he had a trout in a wooden tub, and not enough wood to keep warm. I gave him a sweater and he gave me an angel that still hangs above my door. He died with the reputation of a lunatic and I remember him fondly. If Mr. Chvala met a talking snake at Libín, what happened at Tetín was no less unfathomable. I am relating this story, too, as I heard it firsthand.

*   *   *

Above Tetín lies a hill called Damil and, according to the chronicler Hájek, Teta—one of the daughters of Krok—used to go there to offer sacrifices to the goddesses. A tourist pamphlet from the 1950s still describes a "site of pagan worship" at Damil, and later maps show a fortified settlement. The archeological evidence, however, does not seem to support either of these possibilities. Damil is just a conspicuous hill above an important settlement. It has been damaged by a system of deep quarries in which several caves were found. I believe it must have been in the winter of 1990 when the Tetín speleologists uncovered the so-called New Cave at the bottom of the Modrý quarry. It's an extensive karst cavern that was blasted open sometime in the late 1940s. To keep it from interfering with mine operations, its entrance was filled with about two truckloads of gravel and covered with an iron plate. Over time, falling stones had concealed the plate, so that no one knew where the cave lay. Only a local well sinker who knew how to work with a divining rod was able to help. The speleologists removed a layer of stone, picked out the gravel, and continued their survey.

The New Cave is a dark corrosion hole of an irregular and gloomy shape, and about three hundred meters in length. It has no dripstone decoration. It consists of a system of large domes that were flooded with water and connected through narrow openings. We visited it shortly after it had been rediscovered. There was still snow outside. Someone had dragged an old sofa from the dump to the chasm-like entrance, and lounging on it was a mud-covered speleologist. We climbed down and bustled about in a space that had been closed by a lake in the 1940s. After about two hours I sat down in a cleft that protruded eastward from the rear dome. I had nothing to do, so I turned off the light. It's hard to describe what happened next, because it was neither a vision nor an impression nor a dream. It is as though something was suddenly right in your mind without stimuli coming through any other senses but touch. What was it that I experienced? It was an encounter with something like a dragon, but it was a completely atypical, noninteractive encounter. I perceived it as a giant stegosaurus, a lizard with scales on its back. The scales left a greater impression in my memory than the animal itself—a sensation of touching rough, slippery scales, which could easily be attributed to sensory deprivation.

This animal, or whatever it was, moved through solid rock as if it was air. It just moved and had no idea it was passing through something like rock; it took no notice of it. And now comes the most interesting part: the thing gave the impression of complete foreignness—such as when you say "it was from out of this world" and really mean it—an indifferent and inscrutable foreignness with which it was impossible to communicate. You can talk to an elephant, for example, because you can guess where it is going and why. It is more difficult to communicate with fish in an aquarium, but in this case we understand that the fish were not made for it. It is impossible to say it was too complex or that it had a mind like a mirror—something passed through this place that was so foreign that you can't even use the words *mind* or *complexity* to describe it, because these terms are from our world. Even this story is a simple one: I met something that appeared like a dragon to the mind, but not to the eyes. The encounter was not frightening; the shock came from the realization that there are things with which we have no common basis in space, time, or concepts. Our universe is not necessarily as anthropic as we think.

In retrospect I think the cave at Damil, which has probably existed since the Miocene, is some sort of preserve of the fossil noosphere. The human psyche is extremely expansive; not even in the wilderness are there places where it has not been present. As it expands, it pushes out the nonhuman phenomena, which lose the opportunity to make themselves felt. Only somewhere in the fissures of a certain noosphere do we catch a glimpse of another one. How many of them could there be?

*   *   *

It is easier to have visions than to cope with them. I believe that if one truly longs to understand something, studies and works hard, and if it is something that cannot be achieved through mere work and reason, then the solution will come in a flash through an experience or image. A vision is not a shortcut. A real vision is rare and unpleasant, because by emanating from outside our normal experience, it calls into question our own ingrained reality. It tends to be destabilizing, as well. My friend Vladimír describes it as follows: "I felt like I'd been divided, split as if with an axe, and when I began to grow together again, the pieces connected differently than before."

A Beneficent Story About the Dead and the Living, Two Peacock Feathers, and Eternal Life

He tells me: when you see your own death and survive, it always means a new beginning. Something old is dying and you're being informed of it in a dream or some other shocking experience, because you still have to finish shaping the new thing. The future is not born as something in particular; it is just born. How you are going to take care of it or what you are going to nurture it into is more or less your own affair. But in order to find out that precisely this or that is expected of you, first the grim reaper will begin to whet his scythe right by your ear.

He continues: usually it's not worth it to preoccupy yourself with your dreams too much. The important ones will make themselves heard, and if you don't get it, they'll repeat once or twice. But usually it becomes clear to you that you've experienced something important, and that what stayed above the sieve of everyday consciousness can be left for the birds. One lady took such pleasure in the deep dreamy states of her soul that she went crazy with a copy of Jung in her hands. Then she underwent that psychotherapy she had always liked so much, and almost as a punishment she had to take notes on her dreams, but now she didn't enjoy it as much.

Sometimes it is better not to interpret dreams, because their message is more of a feeling than an explanation. Sometimes it's better to be still and marvel than to understand something halfway. You say, "I'm sitting in a deep ditch on a brick wall." On one side there are new bricks and on the other there are old ones. The wall is a bit unsteady and there are holes in it. Then comes the slightly superficial teacher who actually once caught a glimpse of something remarkable and imparts this in his discourses on mythology. You realize: "Uh oh, he's going to knock over the wall." And sure enough—clumsily and unwittingly, yet pointedly—he does just that. Fortunately, someone outside shouts, "It's okay, the teacher has a pile of bricks in his yard; we'll build a new wall." You have no way of knowing, but in the real world, your teacher really does have a pile of bricks in his yard, because he has been reconstructing the attic. I was there; I talked to him about whether Josef Florian and Martin Putna* were prophets or just wackos. "Luckily a bit of both," he said. But back to the dream.

---

* Josef Florian (1873–1941) was a Czech book publisher and translator who published almost three hundred books and pamphlets, often with original graphics by some of the most prominent artists of his time. Martin Putna (b. 1968) is a Czech literary historian who concentrates on Catholic literature of the nineteenth and twentieth centuries.

He says: I know what's going to happen, and so I'm going to tell you how a psychoanalyst might (possibly) look at it: the wall with its holes divides the worlds of the living and the dead. Sometimes it falls down and the two worlds blend into one another. The dead have always brought turmoil, and so year after year, over many generations and in many cultures, someone is continually repairing the wall. The wall is at the same time shoddy and impermeable, and bricks keep falling out, creating openings. Luckily, unlike Pink Floyd, your teacher not only tears down walls but also maintains them. You know the saying: a good fence makes a good neighbor. He says: but you were at a point in life when almost anything might have brought down that wall. I knew a guy who made it to the wall as a child, because his parents made him recite Karel Jaromír Erben's "Svatební košile" (The wedding shirts). Children experience this differently, like another life. It was not a happy memory for him. But you experienced something so beneficent, at least as I see it, that I wouldn't be surprised if you ended up in a monastery of some sort.

Let's recapitulate: you keep walking and then you meet her. Deborah. We were all profoundly affected by her death, although not everyone is fortunate enough to die in the embrace of what they loved, as Erazim Kohák put it. She died in the wilderness, and it took them a long time to find her body. Each day of the search revived our hopes. For a week we oscillated between inconsolable grief and waiting for a miracle. Strangers came to inquire. The week was completely disrupted at the university. It was rare to see three hundred students experience the loss of someone with such intensity. Even people who only knew her a little asked and cried. A superficial preacher would say, "It was God's will; it was meant to be." And both you and I, for whom certain wounds don't heal, may say the same thing from a different perspective: there was something purifying about it that rose above the grief—that went beyond one person, one family.

So you meet Deborah. You know she's dead, and she knows you know. There's a deeply joyous understanding between you. Something between beauty, grief, and consequence. You're holding a bunch of peacock feathers in your hand and want to give her one. Even now you can recall the colorful, self-contained rainbow of peacock eyes. She hands it back to you gently and says, "You know, here we don't need these things anymore." But you look at it, and then select the biggest, most beautiful feather from the bunch. She holds it like a palm branch. You have exchanged peacock feathers and it was very beautiful. Finally Deborah utters something like a testament, "I wish peace to all people and want everyone to be happy." In the moment it sounds immensely sublime, but if you told anyone about it, it would just be banal. Maybe until a linguist tells you that the Czech words for "happiness," "part," and "participation" derive from the same root.

For centuries of European culture, happiness meant "to be part of something." But let's not speculate too much. Marissa from Vancouver (her parents were from Tuscany) told me that in Canada if you get a peacock feather, it means death. Let's leave aside the question of how peacocks got to Canada, and let's not be frightened by death; it's more of a *vita nuova* for us. To the ancient world, a peacock was a symbol of the soul and eternity. Peacocks lose their feathers, but grow them anew every year like a phoenix. When thinking about eternal materials we tend to think of something made of nickel-chromium steel or red Aswan granite. Our eternity is just durability. In reality, the stuff of eternity is soft, supple, and colorful—something that is not durable, but continually renews itself. The first Christians considered the peacock to be a symbol of eternal life, and the colorful circles of its feathers a symbol of the harmony of the universe. The peacock was depicted as it drank from the life of Christ in the form of a chalice or grapes. Only at the end of the thirteenth century did it become a symbol of vanity and conceit.

And he continues: I analyzed your dream and visualized it. I shivered with joy and was so excited I couldn't fall asleep. I may be wrong and I'd hate to be one who spoils miracles by explaining them, but I'd say that what occurred between the dead and the living is somehow connected with the sacrament of salvation, where it's not your deserts that count, but relationships; not the past, but what is yet to come. Usually people encounter one of the images of their soul and everything takes place inside, but here, in this unique and improbable experience, it seems as though you encountered something even more real, something that affects the life of the community and changes a family tragedy into a public celebration.

The Dual Character of the Sudeten Landscape

Postwar immigrants can never be certain whether the gods of the Sudetenland are with them or against them. They're cautious and don't like foreigners. They're constantly afraid that someone like themselves will come. What if such a person were to drive them out of their homes? After all, the people who lived here before them were sent away, utterly defenseless, by some political power to a distant land where they were afraid to go. They gaze out of their windows searching for the character of a foreigner. They're cautious and impenetrable, and fear strengthens their one-sided shrewdness.

The forgotten poet Jan Opolský* from Nová Paka spoke about a region of two postures: "this region could have two faces: one which blindly injures, another which heals the wounds."

And you realize virtually everywhere in the Sudetenland that you're living on some boundary between foreignness and violence on the one hand and tranquil solace on the other. What is the character of the wound? It's a lack of forgetting in a region where it's never been easy to earn a living. In aerial photos of the Tachov area from 1947,

---

* Jan Opolský (1875–1942) is a now almost forgotten minor Czech symbolist poet.

it's almost impossible to discern any fruit trees. They always bring a certain sweetness to the landscape, a certain healing. It wasn't so long ago that the Hussites withdrew from here. In this cold region wounds don't fester, but nor do they heal very well.

On the other hand, what is the character of the healing? People have been living here for three generations already and for the last one it's become home by right of ancestry. The first and second generations took more than they gave, but the third generation gives and the landscape returns in kind. It is these years in which the pendulum of the Sudeten landscape is shifting from the posture of a wounded region to a healing posture. We can see this almost everywhere in south Bohemia and the Ore Mountains, but far less in the Moravian Sudetenland. Between Nízký Jeseník and Český les there is a difference of maybe ten, twenty years.

In the middle of August 2008 I was in Pernolec at a concert for the Sudeten landscape. Maybe a thousand people came and you had the feeling of being at some sort of Pernolec Woodstock. People met, greeted each other, had a beer together, and then warmed themselves by the fire. You viewed it as a bandage, a small propitiatory cross woven into the landscape here. You could feel how the region—at least at this moment and in this place—was coming together. In a few years it'll probably be a different, still somewhat gloomy country, but more open and friendly.

Hazmburk

Adam says: I had a dream that I was Ishmael and had to find the seashore, but I got lost among fields where haystacks were burning. In the darkness above, illuminated by reflections, there was a great peak from which two towers rose—one white and the other black. It was Hazmburk and I may have been dreaming about Karel Hynek Mácha,

Pavilion at Karlovy Vary

who could see it from the window of his tiny room in Litoměřice. It was the last castle he saw, because then he helped put out a fire below Radobýl and died, God knows why. After that I wrote down in my diary: "Make a square on faith over the hypotenuse, holes by fleeting hope reduce." But I wasn't sure whether I was talking about this place between the eternally burning haystacks or about my sadness.

Hazmburk is a forward sentinel of the Central Bohemian Uplands. The shape of the hill is similar to that of Trosky or Ještěd, accentuated by the rounded Black Tower, made from basalt and positioned lower, and the square White Tower, made from sandstone and positioned higher. The light sandstone became gray during the 1950s due to pollution from heating plants, so nowadays at the Hazmburk Castle, also known as the Klapý Castle, there are two dark gray towers. The hill is oblong and follows a volcanic vein. Heavy volcanic rocks sink into the surrounding argillite, which they push out, showering the base of the hill with large boulders and threatening houses in the nearby village.

What is Hazmburk? It's mainly either an elevated settlement or a cult site dating from when humans began to use iron. It's a peak surrounded by orchards, below which you can see the perimeter wall of a small town in this impractical and dry place, which was abandoned some four or five centuries ago. We are approaching Hazmburk in a large arc and savoring the always slightly monumental perspective that changes every several dozen steps depending on whether the two towers are converging or diverging in the eye of the wayfarer. Some castles are more beautiful from a distance than up close.

We visit Valečov near Mnichovo Hradiště and Hazmburk in the spring, when the fruit trees are in bloom and spring flowers abound on the small rocky meadows between the basalt columns. We avoid Hazmburk during storms, because the peak functions like a lightning rod in the surrounding flatlands and kills people as if it were sacrificing them to the merciless gods of thunder. Some sacred sites are better avoided.

One can mitigate Hazmburk's dark rockiness by taking a walk along the Ohře River under the old oaks at the Libochovice Château. While Hazmburk seizes us by the right of the stronger, Libochovice will calm us, and the silhouettes of beauty here will again remind us of Arcadia. Those who love rocks and towers, however, can head north to Vlastislav and Košťálová. But burning memories and restless memories will only be tamed by the meadow atop Hradišťany (752 meters), which is embraced by prehistoric bulwarks, the shape of which resembles a heart.

Kratochvíle

Jorge Luis Borges says it's not as important to read books as it is to return to those books that we have already read and enjoyed. There's one nice thing about student field trips—you keep going back to the same places. An ordinary tourist would visit Kratochvíle just once or twice in a lifetime, but we are now returning for the fifteenth time and always in May, which accords with the Renaissance. I have always liked Kratochvíle, but it only got under my skin on my fifth or sixth visit, when we were sitting in the Golden Hall on the first floor of the château talking about the beginning of the proud linear modern era. The wind was blowing against the moat and rays of late morning sun were reflecting off the waves at such an angle that elusive ripples of light traversed the ceiling of the hall, decorated in rich stucco with antique motifs. Here, and then there, and after a while again, as if the château were resonating with the eternal echo of glass bells. The premonitions of muddy carp in the surrounding ponds and the brusque call of a peacock in the castle garden. No deep thoughts, no apparitions, only the crystal being of the moment like somewhere in Tuscany. Smooth elation, similar to Prague's Hvězda* when it's not trying to philosophize.

After 1580 one of the most beautiful Renaissance châteaux in all of Bohemia was built at the former Leptač Manor, surrounded by a game park. It is grand not in its architecture but in its placement in a garden and landscape full of ponds and paths. It's not part of any municipality, it's not on a hill, it's alone and satisfied in the flatlands full of waterways and oaks. Imagine a large, rectangular courtyard and in one of its corners (so as not to be in the way), slightly detached from that heroic time of hunters and warriors, there stands a small church with a gilt interior. The rampart adjoins stables and outbuildings above which a whole city of chimneys rises, resembling Chinese towers—yet each one is different.

In the middle stands a large villa surrounded by a moat that keeps the air cool in the summer. And on warm nights one can go on a scow by torchlight and play Pavel Josef Vejvanovský's** sonatas on blaring brass. Drunken noblemen vomit in the water, which here is called "feeding the carp." The smell of hay drifts in from the meadows and the gray shadow of a startled heron flies over the château. The owners: Jakub Krčín of Jelčany,† Petr Vok of Rožmberk,‡ and Emperor Rudolf II. None of them lived here for long; no aristocrat imprinted this place permanently with his spirit. South Bohemia won in the end, a mild and sweet region whose inhabitants understand the soil, labor, and water. Sweet simplicity persists here and delights children, hunters, and philosophers. The joy of sitting in the garden

---

* Letohrádek Hvězda (Star Summer Palace) is a star-shaped Renaissance château in a large park on the outskirts of Prague. It is vibrant with mythological and symbolic meaning, and despite its size it is one of the most interesting Renaissance structures in the Czech Republic.

** Pavel Josef Vejvanovský (ca. 1633/1639–1693) was one of the most prominent Czech composers of the High Baroque period.

† Jakub Krčín (1535–1604) was a prominent Czech Renaissance engineer who built a complex system of artificial ponds and water channels.

‡ Petr Vok of Rožmberk (1539–1611) was an influential Renaissance aristocrat from southern Bohemia.

lazily leafing through a book on the last descendants of the House of Rožmberk or on ferocious Roland, of chasing out all the jealous gods and observing peacocks, garish hens. How one longs to return for a sixteenth time!

Maková hora near Smolotely

Maková hora (Poppy Mountain) is located between Orlík and Příbram. It's a small and, for most of the year, deserted place that isn't as sacred as large pilgrimage sites, although it does bring one joy, peace, and reconciliation. We slowly climb along a narrow road lined with grayish granite stones, removed from fields that today are no longer cultivated. At the summit we may be stunned by the beauty of the landscape, which has a human dimension and contains the right ratio of people, wilderness, and culture. We realize that one of the most beautiful Czech landscapes lies in the uplands that straddle central and south Bohemia, and that to the end of our lives we won't exhaust its charm.

At the beginning of the eighteenth century, the celebrated architect C. A. Canevalle was asked to design a church and a small monastery for the Carmelite monks. The founder died soon after, however, and the church floundered over subsequent centuries between oblivion and attempts at resuscitation. This might be the reason why the place contains so much landscape, long forested hills, a high sky, deer emerging from the forest in the morning dew, and larks singing in the fields, neither too far nor too near.

The Carmelites, followers of the mystic work of Saint John of the Cross and Saint Teresa of Ávila, tried to construct a monastery and sanctuary, or rather a hermitage, in each province, where the Carmelite brothers could pray and contemplate. While the female branch of the order was concerned with the "female" issues of relationships to Christ, such as the Beloved One and Divine Bridegroom, the male branch was developing the legacy of the Inner Fire and the Quiet Rapture, in which there was a place for the earth and its beauty, for trees and birds. Humans approached the Creator through the created, but usually returned from dark nights of the soul to its joyful beginning.

The atmosphere of the place is simple. It's no complicated Svatá hora with its ambiguous depths. It's no *Castillo Interior*, but merely a lane lined with birches and rowans warmed by the soft autumn sun. Maková hora is more reminiscent of places like Lomeček near Vodňany or the old tree-lined lane behind the Čimelice Château, which the Czech master Mikoláš Aleš used to take to his native Mirotice. There's almost nothing to talk about, but we feel unfettered here and we shake off the burden and intricacies of life.

Svatá hora near Příbram

I think I've been to Svatá hora (Holy Mountain) six hundred times, or maybe even more than that, because I attended a mining school right below the mountain and used to go up there almost every day. And for the past thirty years I've been returning. I've never fallen in love with it as I have with other places, but I've never stopped needing it either.

The core of the complex is a small Gothic church now surrounded by cloisters and lost under orchidaceous stuccos. You can't see it, but it's there. Also a Gothic statue of the Mother of God from Stříbrné hory (Silver Mountains) attributed to the first archbishop of Prague, Ernest of Pardubice, can be found there. The statue is dark, roughly hewn, similar to old folk sculpture. I've heard so many vigorous debates about whether or not it's a Black Madonna! The most famous Black Mother of God in all of Bohemia, which would be fitting in this underground mining region. She could also dwell in Plešivec—

the "Olympus of the region," which is visible from the plateau in front of the church and which, long before the Christian Svatá hora, probably represented another sacred mountain consecrated to different gods. I'm thinking how the three-thousand-year-old votive offering of bronze objects found in Plešivec resembles a votive offering of a silver chantry from local mines that is less than three centuries old. And I know that Plešivec and Svatá hora belong together and that one should go to visit them at least a few times in a lifetime.

The baroque complex of buildings was built by the Jesuits as one of the first "coronations" of the landscape in 1658, and soon became the most famous pilgrimage site in all of Bohemia. It sometimes took ten days for a procession to get here. A cantor set the tone and the pilgrims repeated the words of the litanies hour after hour. At night, they would retire to pilgrim dormitories. If you're going to sing religious songs six hours a day in the company of people in a similar frame of mind, you'll arrive at Svatá hora transformed and ready. You won't forget this experience as long as you live. You'll make new friends on the journey and maybe find a partner for life. That's what pilgrimages to Hora were like!

Behind the cloisters and the corner chapels, somewhat to the side, there's a sacred spring resembling a church tower that has sunk into the depths. It's a place of private miracles and curative waters. The cloisters themselves are more of a place of the multitudes and enthrallment, and until now the spirit of Jesuit ideology, albeit beautiful, has been blowing gently through them. The private and the public complement each other in this way, and quiet pilgrims remain to the side. Certain pilgrimage sites accentuate the sanctity of the landscape; others are created in places that are desolate and unspiritual so that they can shine on the landscape. I think Svatá hora is among the latter. It's elevated, but at the same time it draws downward into the depths of underground waters and metals, where the Mother of God in heaven finds her complement in the Black Madonna. In our dreams, we don't

see her among the clouds but calmly floating under water in a dark cavern where she rocks gently with the touch of sidereal currents.

Loket

Loket is best reached through the Ohře Valley from Svatošské skály, but it's best to view the town from the bridge or from an observation point on the road across from the rampart. We stand on the opposite bank and I ask myself, "What should I recount about this town? The polycrystalline structures of feldspar from the coarse-grained granite that Goethe collected here? The Roman rotunda hidden in the Gothic tower or the view through the narrow street to the baroque column? Should one be interested in the underground water conduit and the passages leading from the castle to the buildings on the square?"

Provocative Milton says to me, "Stop it. All the places we visit deserve to be praised and revisited. In all of Loket (with the sole exception of the iron meteorite that once fell here) there's not one extraordinary thing. Loket's strength lies in all its buildings, cliffs, and waters taken together. It resembles Telč in this sense, but Telč is more beautiful than romantic, and lacks Loket's darkness. Set out into the valley in the evening and you may be frightened by a wild hunting ground in the clouds, but that won't happen to you in Telč." He goes on:

> People think they can get to know a city by learning about
> its history and describing its monuments year after year,
> piece by piece. This is a big mistake. We understand cities
> like Loket through observation. We know nothing; we're
> sitting somewhere on a rock, looking across a valley, eating
> a snack and observing the city. Some cherish knowledge,

A Station of the Cross, Římov, Bohemia

but we are developing the skill of *observation*. Knowledge is from people, but observation is most probably from God. You sit and you understand. I think some of us have seen the eternal city in a dream but have forgotten it. And now in every beautiful town like Loket, Úterý, Rabštejn, and Slavonice, they see fragments of their dream and are reminded of it. These are the invisible cities that Marco Polo recounted to Kublai Khan and that were described by Italo Calvino. And it's more than if they knew the history of these cities' houses and palaces. But a place you have observed and made sense of will dig its claws into you and not let go until you have come to know it. So in the end, you won't escape all those family lines who have lived here, all those names and dates, but it will be a foam of days on the solid core of the invisible city. Don't do it too often, though, or you'll be dragging around dozens of little velvet paws dug into your skin with their fine claws.

We're standing on a bridge over the Ohře and talking in a way that wouldn't even cross our minds were we in Karlovy Vary. The sun is setting and goats on a rocky spit of land are nibbling away at the last tufts of grass. Evening is setting in. We take into our hand—as once the great poet did—large phenocrysts of igneous feldspars formed from granite in the shoulder of the road. No, we're not going to read Goethe tonight; it's enough that today we lived his day. The traffic is dying down and the sound of the river is becoming increasingly easier to hear with the deepening night. The sound of water is making its way from the edge of the town to its center. It fills us with gratification.

Kaznějov

Kaznějov, Chlumčany, and Horní Bříza have a lot in common. They have significant deposits of ceramic raw materials, especially kaolin, which gave rise to several industrial sectors during the last third of the nineteenth century. Kaolin was used not only for the production of porcelain but also in paints and as a paper-filling agent. There were even times when air-float kaolin was added to chocolate, and may have been its healthiest ingredient. Grayish and colored kaolin clays were used for making tiles.

Kaolin has one unusual quality—for final products to be really beautiful, it has to be delicately molded or painted. The success of a porcelain manufacturer thus depends not only on the quality of the raw material but also, and primarily, on the skills of its designers and artists. It often happens that the sentiments of these artists are reflected in their entire surroundings. This can be seen in château collections, the design of large gardens, and painted porcelain plaques in cemeteries, as well as in the artistic spirit, which probably dwells in such places because the local people have become accustomed to using beautiful objects.

In former times, kaolin was mined using shafts and tunnels. In some places the tunnels have become large chambers, such as those that still can be found today in Nevřeň, north of Plzeň, or cylindrical ones. The first kaolin wet processing plants were extremely simple—they consisted of long troughs with sand settling at the top and kaolin at the bottom. Kaolin containing a lot of quartz sand was used, for example, for kitchenware or for bulky products in general, but pure white and viscid kaolin was used for the production of decorative objects. Quality products can often be identified based on how the artist works with light. Even purely white objects can make a vivid impression thanks to a texture created by reflections of light on surfaces oriented in various directions.

At an art workshop at the monastery in Plasy, Dutch artists once pointed out a color which is so ordinary for us that it's become commonplace; for them, however, it was characteristic of Bohemia and extremely beautiful. This color consisted of the yellow ocher shades that were created in Plasy and elsewhere from the burnt ferrous ochers found in the vicinity of kaolin deposits. If we compare this color to contemporary colors, we notice a certain animation; although modern colors are pastels and completely homogeneous, they are at the same time boring and bland. My friend Vladimír thinks this is because the old ocher and lime colors contain relatively large sand grains. The color will fade a little due to rain; grains of quartz will protrude above the surface, and attract and reflect light unevenly. The façade of the house changes according to the time of day and the season.

White kaolin thus teaches a similar lesson to that of white baroque statues—to understand the quality of light. Natural ochers help us differentiate between living and dead colors. Beauty is indeed in the eye of the beholder, in the heart of the discerning, and in the movement of unimpressionable light.

Vltava Meadow and Lipno

Hardly any mountains in the Czech border regions have the shape of proper mountains; rather, as in Šumava or the Ore Mountains, there are mainly plains. The topography, in fact, is similar to that found in the middle of the Czech lands, but orogenic movements have lifted it a few hundred meters higher. We approach from the lowlands, ascend into the mountains, and suddenly—what a surprise! We find ourselves on a hilly plain so very similar to the one from which we have just come.

The upper flow of the Vltava actually runs through flat land even though it's located eight hundred meters above sea level. It meanders through the flat Vltava furrow, the lower part of which is flooded by the relatively shallow Lipno Lake, and creates a system of blind branches, bogs, and marshes that are among the most valuable things that can be seen in Šumava. Other than the Třeboň area, it's the only place in our country where moose can be found. A white-tailed eagle or lesser spotted eagle may fly overhead, or a lost heron or even a common eider. The marshes abound in mountain pine and fragrant wild rosemary. Red cranberries glitter underfoot as if you were somewhere in the Russian taiga. But most mysterious are various mud mushrooms, such as Russula helodes.

When you look at a map of Šumava extending to both sides of the border, you will notice an enormous difference. On the Austrian side small hamlets and secluded dwellings lie almost in sight of one another, while on the Czech side you can walk for kilometers through a wilderness devoid of humans. The expulsion of the German-speaking population was a tragedy for people, but nature made use of it to make an inconspicuous return.

The land is strong here and not tamed like the terrain down in the lowlands where it has been touched and transformed by people for at least two or three millennia. The wilderness around us awakens the wilderness within us, so the tales here are cruel and the demons especially dangerous. There is a story here about a man-eating tree that devoured a woodsman, and only a small trickle of blood exuding from a crevice in the bark remained of him. Perhaps in primordial times similar legends were recounted in central Bohemia as well, but the cultivation of land also did away with apparitions, which faded along with their frightfulness.

The common visitor will probably not glimpse the lesser spotted eagle, the strange mushrooms, or even an ordinary savage man, but he or she will see the moss and multifarious stones that, freely flowing in dreams like a boat on a silent mountain stream, accompanied local native Adalbert Stifter* on his way to Vienna. So powerful is nature here that those who were born here or who have lived here for a long time will never forget the rounded stones covered with lichens, the uncertain earth underfoot, the shriveled bark of longleaf pines, or the silence on the dead meadow.

České Budějovice

I have been sitting and waiting for my students for seven hours now. The best way to get to know a place is to be bored there, because the curious mind will eventually begin to probe the surrounding space. Another classic technique for getting to know the genius loci of a place, aside from bored idleness, is to read a book on a nearby fortification. Your mind will open up to the plot and with it your surroundings will enter as well. When you close the book, the place will still be resonating within you.

And so it occurred to me that it's very difficult to be a cursed poet in České Budějovice, compared with Krumlov or Prachatice. The city is tranquil and insufficiently dramatic. Like the majority of the planned colonization cities of Ottokar II, it resembles a large chessboard in which everyone can get lost for a while and find their own little nook. What's majestic about the city is its ground plan and the will to tear out the marshy land on the confluence of the Malše and Vltava Rivers from the flooded meadows and build a royal city on them, which could face down the whole Rožmberk dominion.

South Bohemian brooders, poets, and mystics lived in many

* Adalbert Stifter (1805–1868) was an Austrian painter and writer born in Czech Šumava. His work has a simple natural beauty, but with an undertone of catastrophe. He influenced W. H. Auden and many central European writers.

strange backwaters, but they avoided Budějovice. Tábor is strong and problematic, Písek is mild and sentimental, Krumlov is deep and perhaps tragic, but Budějovice is a place where one builds a house, sends the children to school, and goes to bed in the evening. It is not a city of lunatics and quaint characters, but of orderly townspeople, skilled craftsmen, and the petite bourgeoisie.

It's a nice city, but boring like Austria. There's quiet here for work, but no unrest or inspiration. It's pleasant to stop here, have a Budvar, and stand on the square for a while. One of the most beautiful things in all the city is the gentle knoll that rises almost invisibly from one edge of the square to the fountain, at the top of which Samson is wrestling a lion. Another important place is Dominican Square with its asymmetric saltworks and the monastery that Albert Camus visited on his way to Vienna. At the time, he was thinking about writing a drama called *Budějovice*, as he was attracted by the word *neřest-vice* ("place of vice") hidden in its name. In other words: a horsecar to Linz, the dockyards of Knight Lanna, a beautiful green man in the fresco-covered nave of a church, no Romanesque monuments (the closest one is in Hosín), the proximity of Hluboká, salt and wood, and also the mist over wet meadows at the end of summer.

Budějovice's mediocrity drives out the surrealists and cursed poets to places where beauty or suffering will take their breath away— to Jindřichův Hradec, Prachatice, Chvalšiny, or Třeboň. There's an inscription in the pavement: "Generations come, generations go, but the earth persists."

Český Krumlov (in Wintertime)

In the cold half of the year Krumlov becomes itself. It's late autumn. Visitors are leaving. The city is still its own. It's six in the morning; I'm sitting in the castle courtyard writing a letter to my friend in

Vancouver, a man of letters and an authority on Franz Kafka and Adalbert Stifter. No one else is here. The city and its time surround me. I'm contemplating the notion that in a person normally well protected against the chaos of modern times, cracks appear and windows open, through which images enter.

It's a difficult situation. I'm too solid and focused on myself, but under the influence of the place and possibly also of Stifter and his Šumava companion, Alfred Kubín, I turn into a sort of vapor. I let myself be pulled into a crevice in the wall, where pieces of sentences, fragments of fates, and shadows of loves all live (I would be afraid to fall in love in Český Krumlov). Something was returning me to the bench where I was writing the letter, for the walls were too intimate for me to be able and willing to bear them.

But instead, I found myself in a round rock at the bottom of a river. Fresh, cold water, brown from Šumava's bogs, flowed over me. It knew other stories that one needed not resist. It wandered through fissures in the land, it knew of the mica and feldspar in the mountains, but it spoke the long language of the earth and my hastened time diverged from the deliberate time of the massive stones.

Only in the liquid waters of the Vltava did the two times even up; my mind and the water's mind flowed at the same speed in smooth ripples of gentle whirlpools. We weren't divided in any measure. I could feel the presence of a woman of long ago, the mother of streams, the breath of bears, the pearls of endangered oysters, and peat. And at that moment water began to flow in the castle fountain.

This turned me into a green light, a willow above the river, beeches on the banks, and the light was behind the leaves and vegetation. And again I became solid and concentrated on the letter I was writing on the bench in the courtyard. The difference was that now I heard water flowing. I stand up and go to wash my face. I don't know what else awaits me, but it'll probably be between me, the river, and the trees. I won't share it or reveal myself.

The bears in the castle moat have not yet fallen asleep; they crawl out and bathe in the already cold water. They play like human children; they throw a rotten stump in the air and bite into it. They submerge a beer keg and enjoy watching it rise back to the surface. Brown brothers. I understand their trick. When they're by themselves they act like humans—they are humans, but when they're being observed by tourists they pretend to be bears; that's what's expected of them.

We travel to places like Český Krumlov because certain ideas occur only in particular regions and places. In winter, Krumlov is immersed in itself and in summer it hides from the tourists like a bear. We come here either in early spring when the city is remembering or in the autumn when it is drifting off into dreams.

Jindřichův Hradec

The Gothic and Renaissance towns of south Bohemia are one city with many centers. They join and complement each other. You need to know all of them—even Netolice and remote Bechyně. Without the other towns, you can hardly understand your own. The same applies to these towns as to the polyphonic music of Adam Václav Michna of Otradovice, who lived almost all his life in this town: several voices, but just one composition. This may be because for several centuries the south Bohemian region formed "a kingdom within a kingdom" with its own, essentially self-sufficient economy and culture influenced by northern Italy, while the rest of Bohemia fell more under German influence. There is a big difference between the atmosphere of the clear, melodious, popular yet noble Italian Renaissance and the somewhat stiff, urban beer renaissances from Bavaria or Saxony.

In south Bohemia it's worth teaching your eyes to perceive the colors of frescoes. Oil paints are thick and glossy, and they become black and heavy on old canvases. Fresco paints absorbed in the moist plaster of whitewashed walls allow natural pigments, ferrous ochers, the green of *Genista tinctoria* mixed with alum, enamel paints made from ground cobalt glass, and the brownish red of ground bricks to shine. Frescoes are a different medium than oil painting; they cannot be moved, they belong to the place. It's possible to understand painting and not to understand frescoes. The legend of St. George painted in the castle hall, half painting, half literature, opens the world of the Middle Ages, but the strict character of the preacher in the Minorite monastery is already part of talkative modern times, when God no longer represented a mystery, and the Word changed to words.

Jindřichův Hradec is beautiful on foggy mornings when the haze from Lake Vajgar still shrouds the rising sun. We can best experience the city on an evening walk along the water, under the rampart, and on through Smetanova Street. The best view of the roundel and castle complex is from the other side of the valley. Just sit down on a small wall and gaze across the river, a mere stream and mill gully.

Jindřichův Hradec is a city in which trout jump joyfully above the surface of the Včelnice or Nežárka Rivers in the summertime. The music of the city expresses joy and well-being, but since we're in south Bohemia a contemplative sadness is present as well. The city has its summer and winter face. In the summer they dance here and in the winter they pray. On warm evenings gallant gavottes can be heard from the castle roundel, but on short, cold days we can hear from the Minorite monastery a choir of voices so beautiful that we forget God for the music. The city has something of the seriousness of Český Krumlov as well as something of the seemingly superficial joviality of Telč. It's distinct yet mild like Jičín, and you can escape it, while either Tábor, Bechyně, and Prachatice will absorb and accept you or you'll wage a futile struggle with them for the rest of your life.

A Landscape Where You Can Feel Time

The headquarters of the Czech archaeological team is located in an area of about two square kilometers in Abusir. When the weather is good, one can count fourteen pyramids from here, and an expert can count even more by including the unfinished ones. Abusir is part of the largest burial ground in the world, stretching along the edge of the Nile Valley in a three hundred to five hundred meter strip for at least twelve kilometers. At the same time, it's probably the longest continuously used burial site, with the first burials taking place in the predynastic period and the last in the Coptic period, that is, between the thirty-first century BC and seventh century AD. In addition to people, animals were buried here as well. In one stone tomb opposite our mastabas, some 1.5 million mummified ibises were found; in other places there were tens of thousands of cats, numerous bulls, and at least one shrew buried with a black cubical stone.

It's a landscape where you can feel time. In the past, people claimed to have seen the grayish shadows of the dead and the silhouettes of sacred animals, which then departed for their underground homes. It's a pleasant place and it's quiet in the tombs. The burial ground's atmosphere is addictive. This could be because in Egypt the dead aren't all that dead; they live here in a sort of mysterious community with animals and gods, and sometimes they want to chatter just like modern Egyptians converse in their tearooms. Nevertheless, they're polite and extremely slow. They have difficulty getting used to anything. In life they became accustomed to a certain standard of quality and now they don't want to make any concessions.

Participants in archaeological expeditions clean and restore the half-demolished tombs and gradually gain the shadows' trust. The shadows approach them from time to time and, from the shallowy depths of the underworld, they touch the stripped wires of the collective mind. You're concentrating on some rational, scientific task, but unconsciously you're communicating with the whole mass of the burial ground's collective being, into which most of the shadows dissolved long ago. But occasionally you stop and ask yourself, "Are they sucking me dry or bestowing on me a gift?" I may know the answer in most of these cases. The shadows sap your strength, which, however, is constantly being replenished. But they leave behind an unusual assortment of useless gifts that stay with you for years.

You then feel as though you've received impractical gifts, but you also feel deepened and cleansed from the flow of oscillating time. The abstract concept of "eternity" then becomes timelessness reminiscent of stationary waves in a harbor encircled by levees. The burial ground doesn't carry the burden of time into the endless reaches of the outermost universe; it merely slows it down, almost stopping it.

Certain other landscapes, places, stones, and buildings can do this too. But only in Egypt, under the influence of the more powerful forces of large tombs, pyramids, and fields of mastabas, do we learn to get along with the Elbe Valley region and other landscapes in our own country. If we interrupt the flow of active timelessness, the shadows will stop giving their gifts.

On Landscape Memory   *13*
and the Stone of St. Ivan
at Bytíz near Příbram

Almost every weekend for several years I visited prehistoric sites in Bohemia, Roman churches, and miscellaneous stones of odd shapes. In a forest by Bytíz near Příbram, at the edge of a uranium mine adit, I finally came across a pilgrim stone described by Bohuslav Balbín* himself. For me, it was like discovering a forgotten Mayan temple somewhere in the Yucatán. I realized that stones and various small monuments in general are important vehicles of memory and of a landscape's emotional charge. And since "memorial trees" are recognized today as a category of environmental protection, the same should apply to memorial stones as well.

Landscape and Memory

The landscape of central Europe is as much a natural as it is a cultural phenomenon with respect to its various means of use, such as agriculture—giving rise to the cultural steppe, fish farming,

---

* Bohuslav Balbín (1621–1688) was a Jesuit priest, writer, pilgrim, patriot, and great soul.

grazing in the mountains and foothills, and mining. In many of our protected areas we are not protecting "nature" so much as a specific type of environment stabilized over time and resulting from the interaction of people and their surroundings. Until the nineteenth century and in some places even into the 1950s, human activity had an enhancing effect on the landscape rather than a damaging one. An important milestone came with the Napoleonic Wars, which were followed by demographic growth and the agrarian-industrial revolution, resulting in further population growth in Europe. In particular the introduction of industrial fertilizers and forage clover contributed to eliminating the threat of hunger, led to further specialization in manufacturing, and freed up the labor force for industrial production. The Napoleonic Wars also mark one of the last milestones where the broad masses identified themselves with the intentions of their rulers and willingly accepted a lifestyle of frugality or even poverty. Mass disillusionment has led to an approach—still prevalent today—of attaining the highest possible standard of living without regard for the environment.

Lifestyle, demographic pressure, and only a small number of people directly dependent on the landscape (some 6–10 percent in the European Union, only about 3 percent in the United States) has led to a lack of interest in the environment and to the degradation of entire landscape units. In recent years, however, more and more environmentalists, conservationists, and urban planners have been taking note of the general loss of landscape, which has resulted in landscape protection programs throughout Europe, including the Czech Republic. The aim of this campaign is to point out a phenomenon that Jan Jeník calls the "homeostasis of a landscape" and that Jiří Sádlo describes as "landscape autoregulation" or even the "cybernetics of a landscape's genius loci." In both cases the vehicle is landscape memory. The dictionary *Slovník spisovné češtiny* (1994) defines *paměť* ("memory") as "the ability to preserve perceptions and to recollect them." Sádlo's definition

Rock pile near Landštejn

is even more straightforward: "Memory is the ability to regenerate a former state." Similarly, Jeník considers the homeostasis of a landscape to be "a state in which the main active elements and the main chains of bonds in the landscape system are preserved through autoregulative ecological processes in quasi-stability, and in which no catastrophic reversals take place." A landscape's memory is therefore closely connected to its sustainable life. The Czech word *paměť* is itself composed of a prefix *pa* or *po*, meaning repetition of action or something that happens again and again, and the word *mnít*, meaning "to think" (see Václav Machek, *Etymologický slovník jazyka českého*, 1971). Memory is something repeatedly thinkable and therefore also capable of regeneration; it is something that can rescue us from a catastrophic reversal.

The Main Elements of a Landscape's Memory Framework

1. Topography. The basic memory of a landscape is defined by its topography, which determines in particular the direction of watercourses and an area's water cycle. If the topography changes, for example as a result of coal mining, the landscape's memory is irreversibly lost.

2. Climate and microclimate. These have a fundamental influence on the emergence and development of ecosystems and often also on a landscape's topography.

3. Substrate. The substrate determines and influences the diversity of fauna and flora, and is the vehicle of the microbial environment. The substrate may be completely different from the geological subsurface—examples include calcareous loesses on an otherwise oligotrophic subsoil, and acidic, decalcified sinkhole fillings in the middle of karst plains.

4. Use and care of the landscape. These represent a human investment in natural processes. Memory is evident here especially

in the fact that human settlements are established repeatedly in the same places, in the persistent division of landscape into farmland and forests, and in the maintenance over centuries of the main routes between settlements.

Memory and a Landscape's Emotional Value

We don't always protect the landscape that is of use to us, but we are almost always sensitive to a landscape where we feel at home and that we like. Cultural anthropologists know many ways to achieve that sense of home—one way is to create an optical and spiritual center in a territory, to demarcate its boundaries, to give the landscape microtoponyms, and to populate the landscape with the help of stories and tales relating to a certain place. The mechanism functions in the opposite direction as well—we lose a sense of home where the horizon has been broken, where we do not perceive boundaries (e.g., the construction of a motorway changes one's mental map of a landscape and its demarcation), where microtoponyms and local stories are disappearing. Many local proponents are not consciously aware of this much-described anthropological observation, but its existence is confirmed by environmental initiatives and publications distributed in local museums. There are many regional publications focusing on local tales, chapels, wayside crosses, and memorial trees.

Similarly, we see that one of the main motifs of numerous events organized by environmental initiatives, whatever their rationale, is preserving a sense of the landscape of home. If we analyze this sentiment based on the canvases of landscape painters or photographs of the Bohemian landscape, we notice several basic motifs. These are the field path, cross or wayside shrine, the cottage on a hill, the field, and the tree planted by a human hand. Especially edifices such as small chapels, reconstructed springs, or a linden tree in the fields are places where we discover and experience landscape through human intervention. These are places of contact between the world of humans and the world of nature. We are right to devote great attention to them, because our relationship with the landscape very often begins through them.

At the same time, it is important that the character and beauty of the central European landscape should emerge through its intensive use, that the beautiful and the practical (today we would say the ecological and the economical) should not stand in opposition, but should complement one another. Adalbert Stifter in his story "Der beschriebene Tännling" (in *Der Hochwald*, 1841) writes:

> In the depths beneath Skála, the inhabitants of Horní Planá have vegetable patches in the sun where they grow cabbage from early in the spring and later replant the seedlings in the fields. It is not known why people chose this place, so distant from their abode, but it has been like this for centuries. People simply say that their cabbage, when planted anywhere else in the fields, is not as good, and their attempts to plant seedlings in their gardens down in the village have turned out badly, with the seedlings later dying in the fields. . . . The sun shines all day long on the rocks, so they accumulate warmth and retain it longer than in any other place.

This excerpt is an apt description of persistent experimentation with the landscape and determination of its long-term economically and ecologically usable bounds. And this is possible only in a landscape with a lasting memory. From the point of view of the present day, finding a small field between the rocks high above a village in Šumava would present a riddle—without Stifter's text we would never discover that it was used for growing cabbage seedlings.

Memorial Stones

Monument preservation relies on concepts like "landscape monument" or "historic site." Similarly, environmental protection uses the expression "memorial tree" and understands it to refer to an old or significant tree that is somehow putatively or historically connected with famous moments of Czech history, famous personages, or folktales. I believe that memorial stones deserve to be treated similarly. They are usually small natural stones or rocks, only slightly modified by human activity, and are connected either with historical personages and events or, more commonly, with local superstitions or a folk cult of saints. Examples of such stones include prehistoric upright stones such as Bába near Drahomyšl and Zkamenělý pastýř (Petrified Shepherd) near Klobuky, rock formations such as Lechův kámen (Lech's Stone) in the glacis of the Kouřim fortifications, and stones reputedly connected with historical personages—Sealsfieldův kámen (Sealsfield's Stone) in the Thaya River Valley or Mácha's "Kostničí kámen" near Kokořín.

Another example, and the find which was the inspiration for writing this essay, was the stone of the hermit Ivan in Bytíz near Příbram, which is almost unknown today, but which was visited extensively during at least the last four centuries. The stone lies at the very edge of the territory of uranium mine adit number sixteen, the site of one of the largest forced labor camps of the 1950s, and I therefore would have considered its survival improbable. It's a flat, irregular, triangular, granodiorite boulder 120 centimeters high and 5 meters long of a peripheral type of central Bohemian pluton. The pluton protrudes here as a faulted slope elevated above the contact-metamorphosed Proterozoic rock. The extent of uranium mineralization is linked to a contact zone several hundred meters wide and fractured by transfer faults creating early Variscan carbonate veins. The contact is mineralized here vertically for almost 1,600 meters, but the most important part of the deposit lies about 1,000 meters below the surface. The stone of St. Ivan lies at the foot of the peak traditionally called the Peak of St. Ivan, where several gold mines associated with the short silicious veins and placers were located between Bytíz and Dubenec. The whole area is known as Staré hory (Old Mountains) and its mining boom took place before the nineteenth century. Auriferous mines were still open in 1915, but with no significant success. Today, the hill's surface is covered with small granodiorite rock formations and boulders, as well as shallow furrows following the auriferous structure.

A 3-meter granite cross with a foliage ornament, the inscription "S. IWAN" and the year 1829 decorates the stone. Several crosses and monograms probably dating from the nineteenth century are engraved in the stone. It is evident in places that prie-dieux of a sort had been affixed to the stone. Two half-open rock basins are curious features of this stone. On the western side, a slightly modified half basin measures 50 centimeters in diameter and is 40 centimeters deep. Beneath the cross, in the stone's southeastern corner, is a continuous, two-part, half-open depression 90 centimeters wide, 35 centimeters deep, and 140 centimeters long. This depression, in which one can lie down comfortably, inspired the legend that St. Ivan rested here, although traces in stones in general are usually attributed in Czech folk tales to St. Vojtěch (Adalbert) or to devils.

These features of the stone were well known to Bohuslav Balbín, who described the stone thoroughly:

> In the direction toward Bytíz, there is a deep forest with huge
> trees and a dense oak wood with bristling rock formations.
> It is known for its wildlife, especially herds of boar that
> wallow in its marshes in summer and autumn. In the middle
> of the forest a massive rock rises up in the form of a cross

and triangle that has been visited by processions for ages. One great cross and many others stuck in the ground there lend a touch of the sacred to the area. People call the place the stone of St. Ivan, a name given to it by their ancestors. Ivan is said to have resided at this rock, and lingered a long time spending day and night in prayer. Quite a few traces of his activity are visible on the stone. The stone is differentiated, which is the work of human hands, so you can lie comfortably in one spot [the large basin], sit and read in another [the small basin], and pray in a third. In short, you are comfortable whether lying or sitting. I tried it out myself.

It's a very strange feeling—to take Balbín's *Miscellanea* and sit in the places where he, too, sat centuries before, to share the same space, albeit in a different time.

The Framework of Landscape Memory

In a landscape as a natural and cultural phenomenon (Simon Schama in his celebrated work *Landscape and Memory* even shows that there is no culture without landscape), we need to preserve not only the framework of ecological stability but also the structure of memory. This is determined by natural conditions and by the ways in which the landscape is used by us. While in the nationalistic nineteenth century, medieval castles (as the legacy of a proud, knightly past) and romantic cliffs (as local analogies to the Alpine landscape) took center stage, the focus has been shifting particularly in recent years to memorial trees, stones, chapels, and prehistoric edifices. We are observing a shift from a nationalist understanding of landscape to one that is ecological, harmonizing, and mythical. Consequently, the same attention devoted to memorial trees should be afforded to memorial stones, historically reconstructed springs, fortifications and upright stones, combinations of freestanding statues and trees, and small sacred and profane objects sensitively planted in the landscape. This is where our emotional attachment to the landscape of our home often begins, and it ultimately develops into a more balanced relationship with our environment.

A Brief History of the Twentieth Century
from the Perspective of the Vacated Municipalities near Temelín

South Bohemia is a strip of land composed of three uneven layers. The southern fringe touches the high plateaus of the Šumava Mountains and their rolling foothills. People from here look to Bavaria and Vienna rather than to distant Prague. The middle strip is formed by fertile agricultural basins, wide valleys, and rolling country stretching from Třeboň through České Budějovice and Netolice to Písek and the Otava River watershed. It's a sort of wealthy central region, where people made their living in agriculture and moved away for work less often than the inhabitants of either of south Bohemia's peripheral regions. It used to be a land of old settlers and loudmouths who had a predilection for decorated farmhouse gables, annual markets, and their pastor. The northern, or rather northwestern, strip of south Bohemia touches the rolling country of the Bohemian interior and its southern part gradually merges into the Bohemian-Moravian Highlands. The brown, originally forested soils are rockier and less fertile. The region begins to smell of poverty and forest. Prague lies just beyond the hills.

Temelín* is located on the border between the central and northern strips in a gulf of agricultural lowlands that stretch out from České Budějovice and gradually disappear like a wedge between the Písek Mountains to the west and a strip of forest that hems the Vltava Valley to the east. In such a constellation of landscape, Temelín is positioned in a place that historically lay detached; if one had reason to come here, however, one had only to take a short detour from the important prehistoric Bechyně Road or from the later Imperial Road leading to Písek. It used to be a place that was far and near at the same time.

In 1919, František Vrzák was born in this region. In those times when there was no radio or television, people used to talk with each other a lot and mull over decades-old stories. Children listened with interest, soaking up tales of a bygone era. In modern times, the smartest children leave the countryside for good to study in Písek, Budějovice, or even Prague, but at that time thoughtful people used to stay in the countryside. They grew up into all kinds of wiseacres and smart alecks who would otherwise have found work in the city as lawyers or doctors, but especially in south Bohemia and the Bohemian-Moravian Highlands they became small inventors, brooders, and chroniclers. They read only a few books, but poverty and a current of oral history made them into judicious observers of the surrounding world.

František Vrzák, a late south Bohemian chronicler, wrote of his region and time from the end of World War II until the beginning of the third millennium. The history of political parties, pacts, and significant speeches is well known to historians, but we generally know little about what people in the countryside thought and how they perceived the repercussions of major events. Their relationship to the soil and to domesticated animals was far more important than their relationship to the political situation. Soil was the basis of every-

---

* Temelín is a village in southern Bohemia close to České Budějovice, where a nuclear power plant was built in 1985–2002.

🥨 *Ceiling reflected in holy water font, Kladruby Monastery*

thing. People did not sell their land even in the worst of times. Over those who did hung an omen not merely of bankruptcy, but of utter damnation. It was as though they had neglected or willingly cast away divine grace and doomed all subsequent generations of their family to the life of a person without a home. Similarly, the loss of a cow was viewed as a misfortune, as a life tragedy. Domesticated animals had their own names and their character traits were thoroughly studied. Vrzák saw tears in his father's eyes for the first time in his life when he bought him the new plough of his dreams, which turned the soil. Until 1945, many villages used oil lamps. Soil and a place—two life-long relationships. All year long, children in the countryside looked forward to various fairs. From early childhood they enjoyed sacred sites such as Lomeček near Vodňany and Albrechtice near Týn, with which they built relationships all their lives through marzipan hearts,* family reunions, first loves, and solemn funerals.

That's why there was such a fascination at that time with circus performers who lived in trailers. How can they live without having a home of their own or a piece of land? Who are these creatures who can do so much and have been to so many distant places? The experiences of country people from south Bohemia, like those of other European farmers (as there is only one sky, soil, and grain), make it possible to understand such seemingly different things as circus paintings by Pablo Picasso and many other painters and Marc Chagall's flying cows. Only in Paris do the animals disappear from Chagall's sky of emotional ties, and the figures of musicians, beloved women, and prophets begin to appear more often.

František Vrzák, however, also describes models of behavior during crisis. The 1930s saw a further strengthening of family ties in

---

* It was once a very common practice to bring one's children, spouse, or friends mar-zipan hearts from a country fair, bearing various inscriptions on the hearts such as "to my dearest one." The gift of marzipan hearts served to maintain social relationships and emotional ties. One does not tell one's spouse of many years "I love you"; this is inappro-priate. Instead, one brings a marzipan heart with a message.

the communities. In the country, everyone is somehow kindred to everyone else. Alms were not popular, but people returned favor for favor; they did things out of goodwill for each other, like chopping wood or cutting grass. Such solidarity, cultivated over generations, always emerged when society found itself in crisis. Not even during the war did people snitch on each other. What will the future be like when other crises come as they have for centuries? Will we devour each other or will we find the social wisdom of our ancestors?

And another important observation: the Germans who seized Czechoslovakia at the beginning of the war were viewed as occupiers, but the villagers understood the soldiers because they resembled their sons. When necessary, the villagers helped them, but the soldiers, too, offered the villagers their soup. In south Bohemia, World War II began basically as an encounter between two well-mannered nations who respected certain rules. But the continuing horrors of the time quickly eroded all values and left fear, cruelty, and a petty, hateful malevolence in their place. Only the very old know what they're talking about when they say with a sigh of relief that even though certain things aren't right in public life, thank God at least there's no war.

In 1945 an agricultural cooperative was established in the municipality and Vrzák became its chairman. Food had the value of gold and people had become used to frugality. Politics began to play a role in agriculture. The year 1948 was coming, as were expectations of a happy future and the opportunistic desire to obtain the property of the large estates in the name of a higher Communist ideal. Progress came, but not happiness. The party didn't even have regard for its own people. And so by 1957 even small-scale farmers cultivating less than three hectares gave up their land for fear of not fulfilling the prescribed crop yields. The sanctity of the soil touched by generations had been broken. Two decades later, Vrzák wrote on a piece of paper inserted into his chronicle that people were living more and more for property. No one planted new orchards or expanded bee colonies. The land was losing its value.

In 1980 the Czechoslovak government in Prague decided to build the Temelín nuclear power plant. Vrzák knew the shadow of death had fallen on the region and the people from the six municipalities designated for destruction seemed to him like sheep led by a maniacal shepherd. People became aware of horrible things like forced expulsions only belatedly. The power plant grew gradually and swallowed up more money than had initially seemed possible. People from the surrounding villages departed or were evicted. The last buildings were demolished only very recently, in 1997. The original plans characterized the plant's surroundings as a natural park in the middle of which a nuclear power plant would stand like a cathedral of the modern age. But something else happened, something that may have been more sorrowful for the people, but more congenial for nature.

The desolate land became overgrown with elders and briar and was settled by birds, deer, and hares.

And above, the plant's cooling towers loom in the sky. I've noticed that large industrial buildings like cement factories or power plants give two different impressions—from a distance they blemish the landscape, but when you're inside, you experience a certain feeling of wonder and a sort of indeterminate industrial beauty. I'm not able to take an unequivocal position, as the structure's pros and cons are too closely interwoven. On the one hand, the old agricultural landscape was destroyed and the people were forced to leave. In its place, a power plant was built that we don't presently need, but that will come in handy once the prices of diesel and fossil fuels become unbearable. We may soon be praising nuclear energy because it doesn't emit the greenhouse gases into the atmosphere that change the earth's climate, bringing floods and drought. I feel sadness over the villages in Temelín's surroundings, which since 1948 have been affected by a whole series of burdensome changes and personal tragedies, but I also believe it's still too early to pass final judgment.

On the other hand, I am certain that local chronicler František Vrzák's testimony is not only a history of this derelict "land on the fringe," but also a parable of the twentieth century in central Europe, a parable about the fall of the soil and the rise of the economy and indifference. It's a book that could become part of the recommended school curriculum, as it shows the ordinary, human side of great world events. It doesn't deal with war, tragic death, and a heroic fate, but only sadness, suffering, and people helping one another.

The Six-Cornered Snowflake   *15*

*A snowflake is an ideal New Year's gift for a
mathematician. It looks like a star and comes
from heaven.*
—Johannes Kepler

Are Stars More Reasonable than People?

Johannes Kepler came to Prague many years before a six-cornered snowflake descended on his overcoat in the winter of 1610 somewhere between the Stone Bridge and his home in Jezuitská Street. The next snowflake had a slightly different shape but also six corners, and this was the case for every other snowflake as well. Six corners, the six sides of a cube, the six numbers on a die. Was it just a coincidence or did this number appear in various measures and contexts, once as the heavenly harmony of two orbiting planets and again as a cold white spot on the astronomer's overcoat? What principle selected the number six out of all other possible numbers? It was very disquieting. *For even to Job the Lord said, "have you understood the wealth of snow?"* And another riddle: the snowflake was completely flat, in a material world where everything seeks to assume a three-dimensional shape. If cubes, octahedrons, or hexagonal prisms fell from the sky, it would be more comprehensible than these strange small stars born of the chaos of shapeless water vapor through some unknown force.

Kepler came to Prague in 1600 at the age of twenty-eight. He lived there until the emperor's death, thus a full twelve years, in contrast to Tycho Brahe, who spent only two years in Prague. The two men were incomparable. Tycho's mission was to observe and measure everything that moved in the sky. He had a sharp eye and enjoyed gazing at the stars. He had the manners of a prince, was used to talking to kings, and his house was noisy and full of servants. He had accumulated the largest number of observations ever compiled by an astronomer and was not able to organize them. Kepler, on the other hand, was introverted and quiet. He did not enjoy drinking in pubs; he liked to work in the early morning hours, and preferred peace and solitude. His salary was one-fifteenth of Tycho's and he received it with the same regularity as the miners in Siberian Vorkuta. At the beginning he sent it to his wife, but even later when his family had joined him in Prague he had to work very hard to feed his children as they were coming of age. He outlived his wife—she is buried at the Church of St. Giles, but I couldn't find her grave.

Kepler had poor eyesight, but his mind was extraordinarily sharp. He was clumsy and could not operate Tycho's complicated instruments very well. What interested him was not astronomy or mathematics per se, but the *harmonices mundi*—a set of several simple mathematical relationships by means of which God directs the universe. Magic and mysticism was supposed to use mathematical rules only half-intuitively, the glow of the singing numbers permeating the created space that Kepler wanted to discover. Brahe had no time for Kepler, and possibly also felt the superiority of an experienced practician and man of the world over the overly sensitive, introverted man whose visionary mind was thoroughly concealed by his methodical temperament. Conversely, Kepler had the impression that Tycho was becoming more and more childlike and that he was neglecting science for his social engagements. Brahe's death smoothed over all the differences. On his deathbed, surrounded by his disciples and servants, he begged Kepler to develop his theories further.

At that time the situation in Prague was unique, and not only because of Rudolf II, who was able to support the sciences and the arts thanks to favorable economic conditions in the kingdom. Above all, the divided church was unable to enforce the hegemony of its views, which dominated most of Europe. And then there was silver mining and fish farming. The mines in the Jáchymov area* extended to depths below three hundred meters, and brought difficulties with ventilation and water pumping. The sophisticated and complex transmissions once used in Tycho's astrolabes now found practical application in mining equipment that was able to pull to the surface up to one cubic meter of water at a time. The construction of fishpond systems spanning dozens of miles like the Opatovice Canal near Pardubice, connecting some two hundred ponds, or the Zlatá strouha in Třeboň was extremely demanding in terms of exact height measurements in flat terrain, where only a few centimeters determined the slope of a channel. The precise techniques of land surveying could be applied well in surveying the stars. How different was the approach of Giordano Bruno, who had declared at the Prague Castle just a few years before that the stars were more rational than people, that they had free will and went where they pleased.

---

* Jáchymov is a former mining town in the Ore Mountains of northwest Bohemia that became famous in the sixteenth century as a rich silver mine and later after 1945 as one of Europe's first uranium mines. The German name Joachimsthal can be translated as St. Joachim's Valley, and large valuable silver coins called Joachimsthaler (later Thaler, Tolar, and etymologically also dollar) were minted here. The size and weight of the Mexican and American silver dollars are derived from original local silver coins, and thus Jáchymov is often called the cradle of the American dollar.

Where There Is Matter, There Is Shape—Ubi materia,
ibi geometria

It's a long way from astronomy to a snowflake, but there's a
clear link between discovering the secret symmetry of the universe
and a tiny cold object that not long ago was unthinking water vapor
with no memory. In 1611, Kepler published a short essay of four-by-six
pages in Latin entitled "A New Year's Gift; or, On the Six-Cornered
Snowflake" through Godfried Tampach in Frankfurt. This book is
now considered a fundamental work of scientific crystallography and
is one of the first attempts at a mathematical theory of the formation
of organic and inorganic shapes. Kepler's idea of the closest possible
arrangement of atoms is often mentioned. I don't want to repeat Kepler's thought process here from honeycombs to the seeds of a pome-
granate, which has already been described in so many textbooks on
the history of science. Rather, I'm more interested in the history of
imagination, of the mirror of numbers rotating in space, and the octahedron of the earth's soul projecting the formative faculty that influences every mineral particle, but not the plants, which of course have
their individual souls.

Yet this grand vision of the world as a mathematical machine—
as nonrandom as a Swiss watch—is somehow inhuman. Somewhere
in the *Divine Comedy*, Dante mentions the gears in a clock resembling the planetary system. He means this literally: the clock is not
just a machine for measuring time, it is also a model of the world,
and the fact that it runs as fast as the world demonstrates that it's a
good model. Something like this is how I imagine dictators' dreams
of a clean, smoothly running society; just oil it a bit and clean out the
gunk that doesn't belong. Kepler was far removed from that, however,
as the Thirty Years' War loomed on the horizon. The idea that the
organization of society reflected some heavenly order and could be expressed as a mathematical equation would soon cease to be accepted.

Street in Old Town, Prague

Redefining the universe—as Copernicus, Galileo, and Kepler all attempted to do—would also mean looking at society from a different perspective. Actually, it's not clear to me why, say, Copernicus is mentioned in the history of astronomy but not in the history of sociology. But back to the snowflake and the questioning Kepler: "Why does it have six corners? Who carved out its core? Where does the number six come from and why is it possible to connect the corners in a circle? Heat is everywhere—although it probably has some sort of spatial structure—so why are snowflakes flat and not round?" He watched with wonder ("cum admiratione") as they fell and had the sense that often something holds a snowflake in the air, then it drops down only to float again for a while. And he kept asking: why six and not five or seven? He considered it absurd that every flake should have a soul that tells it what form to don. Thus, there must be some universal principle contained in the earth that influences the snowflake's core, and this in turn influences the shape of the arms. Kepler knew of three bodies that could fill a space completely; besides the tetrahedron, these were the cube and the octahedron. He imagined that some important characteristic of God took the shape of a cube or an octahedron. As I ponder the idea of a cubic God, I see before my eyes not only the attempts of the cubists to iterate artworks to the fundamental shape of the world but also the black Kaaba in Mecca and thousands of Muslims rotating around it. *Kaaba* means "cube" or "hexahedron" and has the shape of a cube, reflecting some particularly sacred characteristic of God embodied in the earth.

> The realm of the soul resembles the shape of a regular
> geometric body and humans with their functions resemble a
> cube. In the body of the earth there is a formative faculty that
> is carried by vapor. This formative faculty not only bears a
> purpose, it is also decorative. Its habit is to play with the flow
> of time, which can be demonstrated in mineralogical samples

that take many different shapes. In God's eternity there are many spirits that are spirits of spaces rather than of surfaces, and thus these spirits must have the shapes of geometric bodies such as the cube.

And I imagine how, in the haunted castle of the National Gallery in the Trade Fair Palace, it is not the milky specter of say Prof. Milan Knížák* that appears, but rather a shining cube, which Kepler viewed as the father of all bodies.

A cube is the shape of giving and going out, whereas the octahedron gathers itself inside, is more compact, can be derived from the cube, but has only six corners. Goldsmiths say that the most beautiful octahedrons can be found in diamonds. The earth, an animal three times larger, has a soul containing various bodies; the earth has locked away in its heart the cube and the octahedron, as well as other bodies. It is possible that the formative faculty in the soul of the animal earth vacillates according to the amount of vapor carrying its influences.

If we attempt to summarize the imaginative and extrascientific part of Kepler's essay on the snowflake, we can state that the soul of the earth must be everywhere where there is water or vapor. In different places not only can its power vary but also its formative faculty—*facultas formatrix*—may emphasize different geometric arrangements. The fundamental and strongest, however, remain the cube and the octahedron. Even the human mind somehow resembles a cube. The earth is an animal and, moreover, a tripartite animal with a heart and

---

* Milan Knížák, a former director of the National Gallery, is a controversial, sometimes hated figure of Czech contemporary art.

a glowing soul. Johannes Kepler does not allege any of this, however; he merely asks and the answer is not clear to him—and in the end he defers the entire issue to the chemist, who should be able to understand it better than he.

The History of the Snowflake

Already by sometime in the second century AD the Chinese had noticed that snowflakes have six corners, whereas plants and trees tend to be pentamerous. The European literature on snowflakes begins with a statement by Albertus Magnus (circa 1260) that snowflakes are star-shaped. Only in 1555 did Olaus Magnus, the archbishop of Uppsala, draw twenty-three snow shapes, but it was Kepler who recognized their hexamerous symmetry. Descartes later emphasized the symmetry of snow anew in *Meteorology* (1635), and drew among the shapes of various snowflakes a quite rare type resembling a spool of thread—a stem of ice with a six-cornered snowflake at each end where the diameters of the snowflake exceed that of the stem. And then works follow in rapid succession: Erasmus Bartholinus, Robert Hooke, Donato Rossetti, William Scoresby, and others publish detailed descriptions of snow crystals. A significant artistic feat is a set of sixty-eight and later ninety-seven wood engravings of snowflakes in the Sekka Yusetsu cycle by Japanese daimyo Doi Toshitsura, published in 1832.

Snow is hexagonal because it reflects the inner structure of atoms, where water molecules bind together to form hexagons with open bonding sites on the sides, and so it is easier for the flakes to grow into flat plates rather than upward or downward. About 80 percent of snowflakes actually have the shape of those Keplerian stars, but the shape of snow depends mainly on air temperature. At negative three to negative five degrees Celsius snow needles develop best, at negative five to negative eight degrees Celsius hollow snow columns grow, and at even lower temperatures we can find thin snow plates and other shapes according to the falling temperature. Snow is so sensitive to temperature that in borderline intervals it is a matter of just one degree Celsius that causes different shapes to fall from the sky. The largest snowflakes have a diameter of around 12 centimeters, while the usual diameter is 2.4 millimeters with an area of 1.3 square millimeters and a weight of as little as 2.3 milligrams, which explains why it falls so slowly. Science can deal with snow at the superficial level of description, but at the level of the geometry of atomic bonds, matter as such becomes a mystery.

As far as everything else is concerned, it's one thing to read about Kepler's ideas* and quite another to imagine how such a world permeated with the faculties of geometric bodies emanating from the soul of the earth would really work. The words make us dizzy. I believe that the animal earth has a heart and influences us, but I don't know what else I should add.

---

* An English version of Kepler's essay was published in a bilingual edition by Oxford University Press in 1966, translated by Colin Hardie. There are three German translations, the last in 1958 by Karl Hugo Strunz and H. Borm under the title *Über den hexagonalen Schnee* (Regensburg: Bernhard Bosse). As far as I know, there is no Czech translation. There are several editions in Latin—Kepler's *Opera Omnia* was published in 1868 (ed. Christian Frisch) and *Gesammelte Werke* (ed. Max Caspar and Fritz Hammer) came out in 1941. The text of this essay quotes Kepler's authentic ideas in several places, but not the exact wording.

A place is a place in the heart; it's a relationship.

More than thirty years ago—I'm almost afraid to write down how long it's been—I started hiking through Bohemia. At that time I was very fond of collecting minerals. A strong desire to discover and possess brought me to small forgotten quarries and later to old mines. I don't want go into the details here of my experiences in such places, which several times almost ended in death. It was a heroic era, and nowadays I think its purpose was so I could learn to work with the earth. When you collect minerals, you get immediate feedback. When you discover—half intuitively and half thanks to your experience—a new or long-forgotten locality, the find itself tells you how well you're working with nature.

After that I spent ten years digging in caves. I didn't need to possess stones anymore; I was surrounded by the elements of the earth. Searching for new subterranean spaces is even more demanding in terms of knowledge and intuition than looking for stones. You become very familiar with clay. When I look back on those years now, I have a strong but not unpleasant sense of wandering in underground realms, the rough feel of rock, and working with soil. And, again, I don't want to talk about experiences; I'm only pondering with wonder

Grates covering adits in the Stag Moat where Russian bears were kept, Prague Castle

the places I once visited, or where I worked, but didn't understand—
for example Propast mrtvých (The Chasm of the Dead) at Tobolský
vrch, where human victims were hurled.* A lack of understanding prevailed generally throughout those years; fortunately, experience, albeit
forgotten, remains.

At that time I visited many villages, hills, and mines where
one normally has no reason to go. I don't know if this is true for everyone, but I need to work in a place, to touch it physically somehow,
to exert a certain amount of effort, in order to be able to understand
it. I'm not able to just come and comprehend; I need to do something, and only in the evening after work, when I look around, does
it become clear where I am. It usually comes through soil, through
rock, or through the earth itself. It's not a bright idea or an all-per-
meating meditation; it blows through the earth and it comes to you,
but not often. I'm patient; I don't need to come, understand, have an
experience, an insight. I'm a wayfarer, not a conqueror. I don't enter
through closed doors. I don't have a jewelry box filled with stolen
secrets.

For the past ten years or so I've been continuously visiting sacred sites, primeval forts, cloisters, Romanesque churches, strangely
shaped rocks, ritual caves, and sandstone ledges with sacrificial sites
almost ten thousand years old. There were times when I wanted to
write a book about these places, because I was aware of how much
they had given me. Today I feel no need to possess stones, to discover
caves, or to write a book about sacred sites. They are here, and many of
them can be found easily—all you need to do is read the legend on the
back of a hiking map. It took me twenty years, shattered knees, and
back pain before I got close to a secret, to the essence of a place. You

---

* The Chasm of the Dead in the Czech Karst represents one of the cave sanctuaries of
the Early Iron Age that people were thrown into, possibly so that they might become
pilgrims and messengers to the underworld gods.

can do it, too; I leave tracks, but I don't show the way to others. I don't see clearly and I don't want to mislead anyone. I don't hoard; I prefer to forget, so that there's space in my mind for things yet to come. I've seen more than I'll ever be able to understand until the end of my life.

I started writing the following text ten years ago after a week of wandering underground between Bristol and Avebury. I'll never forget the unbelievable underground maze in Monkton Farleigh Quarry near Corsham spanning almost fifty kilometers. The long-forsaken underground quarry here led to a huge weapons cache from World War II, full of rusty ammunition. The depth of the excavation and the military tenacity of the British were a good introduction to understanding Avebury. A cartridge with rusty bullets is not as different from a trilithon at Stonehenge as it may now seem to us in different times. Many prehistoric sacred sites are connected with such strange matters that I enter them with the caution of a traveler in an unknown village in the Balkans.

I understand much better those landscapes and places where I was able to get underground, or at least sleep outdoors. The earth will eventually confide the most to those who do not ask too loudly. The best secrets are merely hinted to us, but do not reveal themselves. At that time, below Silbury, I began putting together (for myself) "wayfarer's rules." I finished them two years later in Labské pískovce and then forgot them. Here they are—and they shouldn't be taken too seriously, because the essence of a place and the essence of a person cannot be captured in a single schema.

The Rule of Home

A person is at home in only one landscape. Some people can comprehend two or three landscapes, but no more. Every memory—even the littlest one—of the place where we are at home is more important than a large memory of another landscape. Despite this, however, we need to travel abroad—to be able to compare, to become aware of the smallness of our home, and to realize where we belong.

The Rule of Resonance

A small place with which I resonate is more important than a large pilgrimage site where I am only a visitor.

The Rule of Irreplaceability

There exist places that cannot be replaced by any other places. In our country these are, for example, Vyšehrad, Velehrad, and Říp. There are irreplaceable cities such as Znojmo and Prague.

The Rule of Blowing

A spirit is blown to where it wants to go, but there are places where it wants to go more. Rarely does the "spirit within us" perceive directly the "spirit around us." We are not angels; we need a tangible intermediary—a place or an object. They are deserving of respect, but that which moves them even more so.

The Rule of Various Viewpoints

Some perceive the beauty of a place, others myths or poetry, while others understand electrical charges and energy flows. None of these paths is superior to another. Many say they know where and how a hidden force flows—but this is often only the understanding of a technician who knows how the "thing" is made, where the wires run, without noticing other, equally important (or more important) aspects. Few people are designed in such a way so as to be able to listen to multiple muses.

The Rule of the Lid

Certain places and even whole landscapes are open and friendly; others are covered with a lid—closed or injured and suffering. Underneath, there is perhaps a distorted, but still beautiful inner life—large parts of the Ore Mountains, for example, and of the Sudetenland in general. There are also landscapes like the Czech Karst, whose essence is elusive, concealed in subterranean streams, and only rarely comes up to the surface. You can live in such landscapes for years and not glimpse their spirit. But that doesn't mean there isn't one.

The Rule of Return

Just as there is love at first sight between people, there is love at first sight between a person and a place. Most of the time, however, one must return, observe, and get to know a place. Really strong places may open up for only a few hours a year. One must come here at different times of day and in different seasons. Most suitable are moments when one can no longer recognize clear boundaries of objects—such as in fog or darkness. Certain places (and certain truths) show themselves only when they're not clearly visible. An experience from Avebury: the force as a giant mole slowly makes its way toward the surface and then swerves to the depths and the unknown. I never saw it again.

The Law of the Slow Approach

The idea that it is possible to come by car, stay a while, and understand a place is delusory in most cases. Certain places are timid; others behave like CEOs—they'll receive you, but you'll have to wait. I know one place (surely there are many of them, but I haven't had time to visit them) that one must approach for three days. One should never approach an unknown sacred site directly; it's better to go slowly, hesitate, first walk around the place, and only then come closer. An unknown place is not only a place that we don't know; it's also a place that doesn't know us. Certain places require great respect, while for others this is an obstacle and we'd do better with a smile.

The Rule of Friendly Teasing

If we want to get to know a place, it's necessary to alternate active and passive approaches. In the active part of the encounter, one nudges the place with a question: *Who are you, please?* Then usually nothing happens—the place lives in a different time than the person—and then sometimes an answer follows. Quick answers tend to be misleading.

The Rule of Sacred Games

There are places or lines where unusual things happen and where sensitive people see unusual images. In many cases these phenomena refer to real events and require careful attention. There are many places, however, that are playful or are endowed with a special (sometimes mischievous) humor, and produce images that are not meant to be explained.

The Rule of Culmination

A place that has a spirit matures and grows. It can have several primeval meanings, later a Christian soul, and today perhaps a deeply ecological meaning. There is usually something of nature and something of humanity in these places. Something relatively stable, but also something changeable that addresses each period in its own way. Certain lazy and untidy or bewitched places confuse periods or sleep for ages and then awake into a time in which they have difficulty finding their bearings. Certain places, like a local magnetic field, shift by up to several dozen meters over a few centuries and weaken in turns or permanently.

The Rule of Mutual Awakening

By traveling to places, we awaken and heal the earth, which repays us. A place in the landscape corresponds to a place in the heart.

*   *   *

If it wasn't for this last rule, I probably wouldn't have written this missive. But the awakening earth wishes to be visited. I observe

repeatedly how places in Bohemia are rusty and unused. But they're starting to move. The number of silent wayfarers is increasing. More and more often one comes across little sacrifices on stones and in forests—a bouquet of grain, a bird's feather tied in heather, or a circle made from the shells of snails.

*　*　*

My message is simple. *The gods of the earth are awakening, a time of changes is coming*, I tell myself with joy and trepidation.

৯৩১৯

৯৩ *Tertiary volcano north of Prague*

ACKNOWLEDGMENTS

The author and the photographer wish to thank: Alexander Stipsits, who organized the fine translation by Evan W. Mellander; Pamela and John Lifton-Zoline for their wonderful and continued support; Laurie Olin, who was at the scene when the book was first discussed; and John Dixon Hunt for his immediate enthusiasm. We also thank Henry Hanson for his solid support; Miluše Ždražilová, Tomáš Heczko, and Petr Zidek for help with all the logistics of travel needed while photographing this book; and Jerry Singerman and the staff at Penn Press. The title of this book was inspired by the poem "The Far Field" by Theodore Roethke.

      *   *   *

The Centre for the Future is a not-for-profit institution founded in 2010 by John and Pamela Lifton-Zoline and Alexander Stipsits, in Slavonice, Czech Republic. The Centre was founded to be a space for education, arts, and research, and to promote civil society, cultural landscapes, and the strategies for a sustainable future. Working with artists, scientists, educators, and community leaders, the Centre has developed a number of projects in Slavonice and the region, and various national and international initiatives.

Those of us at the Centre greatly value the opportunity to work with the extraordinary scholar Václav Cílek in support of *To Breathe with Birds*. He exemplifies that grand tradition of humane and rational practice where we readers are allowed the joy of participating in the movement of a hugely curious and refined sensibility as it moves through the vast real world.

*   *   *

"Preface: Gathering Strength and Drinking Dawn in the Landscape of Home," "Walking Through a Landscape," and "On Landscape Memory and the Stone of St. Ivan at Bytíz near Příbram" appeared in the *Hudson Review* 66, no. 1 (April 2013): 97–112.